THE OSLER GUIDE TO COMMER(

THE OSLER GUIDE TO COMMERCIAL ARBITRATION IN CANADA

A Practical Introduction to Domestic and International Commercial Arbitration

First Edition

Babak Barin
B.A., LL.B.
Admitted to practise in Québec, Ontario, Alberta and England & Wales

Andrew D. Little
B.A. (Hons.), LL.B, B.C.L. (Oxon.)
Admitted to practise in Alberta and Ontario

Randy A. Pepper
B.A. (Hons.), LL.B, LL.M (London)
Admitted to practise in Ontario, Hong Kong and England & Wales

165101

KLUWER LAW
INTERNATIONAL

A C.I.P Catalogue record for this book is available from the Library of Congress.

ISBN 90-411-2428-4

Published by Kluwer Law International,
P.O. Box 85889, 2508 CN The Hague, The Netherlands
sales@kluwerlaw.com
http://www.kluwerlaw.com

Sold and distributed in North, Central and South America
by Aspen Publishers, Inc.
7201 McKinney Circle, Frederick, MD 21704, USA

Sold and distributed in all other countries
by Extenza-Turpin, Stratton Business Park,
Pegasus Drive, Biggleswade, Bedfordshire,
SG18 8TQ, United Kingdom

Printed on acid-free paper

Printed in The Netherlands

Contents

Foreword

The last two decades have seen Canada emerge as a leader in the commercial arbitration field. Canada was the first country to adopt the UNCITRAL Model Law on International Commercial Arbitration which has provided the framework for modern arbitration legislation in many countries around the world. Canadian judges have embraced this new legislation and shown a willingness to respect the principles of party autonomy. As a result, Canadian courts have provided a significant contribution to the development of the jurisprudence under the Model Law.

In the midst of these developments, Canadian business has become increasingly global in its reach and outlook. As Canadian businesses have become more involved in transactions with other international players, many have recognized that arbitration is the preferred method of dispute resolution in international transactions.

This Guide began as a proposed commentary to provide in-house counsel and business lawyers with assistance in designing effective and efficient methods of dispute resolution. As interest grew in the advantages of commercial arbitration over conventional litigation, we expanded the commentary to provide a primer on the considerations involved in arbitrating disputes within Canada. As it has evolved, this Guide will hopefully provide readers with a handy and practical overview of the issues presented by domestic and international commercial arbitration from the stage of drafting the arbitration agreement, through the selection and appointment of the arbitral tribunal, the conduct of the arbitration and the challenges to the arbitral award. We have tried to present the relevant law in Canada as at September 1, 2005.

This book would not have been possible without the assistance of many people including countless colleagues, articling students and assistants at Osler. We would also like to thank our families for their understanding and support especially in view of the many weekends and evenings which were sacrificed to the Guide's development.

This book is for Marie-Claude, Nakissa and Noah; Valeri, Jasmine and Priya; and MaryAnn and Naz.

Babak Barin
Andrew D. Little
Randy A. Pepper
December, 2005

I. Introduction

This Guide is designed to provide an introduction to the legal framework of commercial arbitration in Canada. It outlines key considerations in adopting arbitration as an effective dispute resolution mechanism for commercial disputes, and is intended to be a resource text for business personnel, in-house counsel and other legal professionals who are interested or involved in Canadian arbitration proceedings.

There are good reasons to consider arbitration in Canada over conventional litigation or arbitration in other jurisdictions. Since 1986, Canada and its legislators have recognized the importance of commercial arbitration, both domestic and international, and have developed a modern statutory framework that encourages the use of such dispute resolution mechanisms. The legislative reforms of the 1980s and the case law that has followed represent a "shift in policy and attitude"[1] from the legislation and decades of arbitration decisions that preceded them. Canadian courts are now very supportive of arbitration, in that they generally uphold the parties' bargain to resolve disputes through such a dispute resolution mechanism and interpret arbitration clauses expansively. There is no doubt that today, Canada is an arbitration-friendly jurisdiction.

Through this Guide, we hope to encourage a constructive and thoughtful approach to the decision of whether to use arbitration to resolve corporate and

---

[1] *Ontario Hydro v. Denison Mines Ltd*, [1992] O.J. No. 2948, at 3; *Babcock and Wilcock Canada Ltd. v. Agrium Inc.* (2005), 363 A.R. 103 (C.A.), at 106-107 (para. 7).

commercial disputes, and to provide a useful resource for the preparation of arbitration agreements and the conduct of arbitration proceedings in Canada. Because our intention is not to write a comprehensive textbook, we have not attempted to cover all issues, including less common (but often important) ones that may arise before or during arbitration proceedings. We have examined many issues that commonly arise in Canadian arbitration proceedings, based on our experience in the field and the body of decided court cases in Canada. We have also made reference to some of the arbitration rules commonly used in Canada, both in international and domestic arbitrations.

II. What is Arbitration?

None of the Canadian arbitration statutes establishes a comprehensive definition of arbitration.[2] In general, arbitration may be described as a mechanism
for the resolution of disputes in private, pursuant to an agreement under
which two or more parties agree to be bound by the decision of one or more
independent and impartial arbitrators, who, after a fair hearing and according
to rules of law, render an enforceable award.

In the common law provinces of Canada, legislators have defined an
"arbitration agreement" to be "an agreement by which two or more persons
agree to submit to arbitration a dispute that has arisen or may arise between
them."[3] In Québec, the *Civil Code of Québec (C.C.Q.)*[4] states that "an

---

[2] In the Canadian provinces, only the British Columbia domestic and international arbitration legislation includes a definition. The *Commercial Arbitration Act*, R.S.B.C. 1996,
c. 55 defines "arbitration" in s. 1 as "a reference before an arbitrator to resolve a dispute
under the Act or an arbitration agreement." The *International Commercial Arbitration
Act*, R.S.B.C. 1996, c. 233 defines "arbitration" in s. 2(1) as "any arbitration whether
or not administered by the B.C. Arbitration Centre or any other permanent arbitral
institution." The UNCITRAL Model Law (1985) adopted by the other provinces and
in the federal legislation defines "arbitration" in Article 2 as "any arbitration whether
or not administered by a permanent arbitral institution."

[3] *Ontario Domestic Act, infra* note 27, s. 1. A similar definition can be found in the
various domestic statutes of the other Canadian common law provinces.

[4] R.S.Q. 1991, c. 64.

arbitration agreement is a contract by which the parties undertake to submit a present or future dispute to the decision of one or more arbitrators, to the exclusion of the courts."[5]

While both international and domestic arbitration are subjects of legislation in Canada, to date, other forms of dispute resolution are not. It is appropriate therefore to compare arbitration to these other forms of dispute resolution.

A. ARBITRATION VERSUS EXPERT DETERMINATION

Arbitration must be distinguished from expert determination. While both are dispute resolution mechanisms leading to a binding result that may rely upon the decision-makers' expertise, experts are a unique species of dispute resolution provider.

Expert determination is not subject to review by a court in Canada under any legislation. By contrast, arbitrators are subject to arbitration legislation and their decisions are subject to review by way of an application to set aside (or a motion for annulment in Québec) or, where available in the common law domestic context, by way of appeal. As one author notes, the crucial difference between expert determination and arbitration lies in:

> the procedure and the absence of remedies for procedural irregularity in expert determination. An arbitration award may be set aside because the procedure fails to conform to the statutory standard of fairness which is closely derived from the principles of natural justice: no such remedy is generally available to invalidate an expert's decision.[6]

---

[5] *Ibid.*, Article 2638.

[6] John Kendall, *Expert Determination*, 3rd edn (London: Sweet & Maxwell, 2001) at 2. See also the decision of the Supreme Court of Canada in *Sport Maska Inc. v. Zittrer*, [1988] 1 S.C.R. 564, *per* L'Heureux-Dubé, J., at 602-605 for a general discussion on the similarities and differences between arbitration and expert determination or "opinion."

If the parties' agreement does not make the decision-makers' role clear, the function of the person will be very important in determining whether the person is acting as an expert, or as an arbitrator. If the person has a mandate to resolve a dispute between the parties and does so in a manner that has the inherent characteristics of an arbitration, the person is more likely to be considered an arbitrator than an expert. Thus, where the parties are required to present evidence and submissions to an impartial decision-maker, rather than asking the person to carry out his or her own independent inquiries in order to reach a conclusion, it may suggest that the process intended is one of arbitration rather than expert determination. The title of the person will not be a significant factor, unless the parties' agreement makes their intention to appoint an "expert" clear.[7] An expert determination may be carried out by a firm or corporation, such as an accounting or engineering firm. Arbitrators on the other hand must be identifiable individuals.

B. ARBITRATION VERSUS MEDIATION (OR CONCILIATION)

Arbitration must be differentiated from mediation (or conciliation as it is sometimes called). In contrast to the adjudicative function of arbitration, mediation is a facilitative process. It is essentially a voluntary mechanism by which disputing parties engage the assistance of a neutral third party who helps them try to arrive at an agreed resolution of their dispute. Unlike arbitration, the mediator has no authority to make any decisions that are binding on the parties.[8] There are many different forms of mediation, and they cover a variety of fields of activity, each with its own characteristics and conditions.

---

[7] In addition to *Zittrer, ibid.*, see *Re Concord Pacific Developments Ltd. and British Columbia Pavilion Corp.* (1991), 85 D.L.R. (4th) 402 (B.C.C.A), esp. at 413-414 (*per* Legg, J.A.). On the facts of *Concord Pacific*, the court concluded that the person acted as both valuer and arbitrator (at 416).

[8] Henry Brown & Arthur Marriott, *ADR Principles and Practice*, 2nd edn (London: Sweet & Maxwell, 1999) at 127.

Mediation is common in almost all Canadian provinces. Some provincial courts such as those in Ontario and Québec have gained significant experience in implementing and managing court-annexed mediations and settlement conferences.[9] But so far, no real national framework exists in Canada to make the mediation process more certain and reliable for participants, something commercial actors often find attractive. While certainty of process may be desirable, some argue that formalizing mediation in legislation will do more harm than good. The very reason why mediation works and is gaining popularity, they argue, is precisely because it is not structured and regulated.

The United Nations Commission on International Trade Law ("UNCITRAL") Model Law on International Commercial Conciliation ("Conciliation Model Law") may play a critical and persuasive role in resolving this debate. The Conciliation Model Law represents a consensus among the 90 member nations that participated in its preparation and drafting. Adopted in June 2002 by the core legal body of the United Nations system in the field of international trade law, the Conciliation Model Law has 14 articles which offer basic rules for conducting conciliation in international or domestic commercial disputes.

In an effort to remain consistent with and benefit from the experience of the UNCITRAL Model Law on International Commercial Arbitration ("UNCITRAL Model Law"), the Conciliation Model Law defines the terms "international" and "commercial" in essentially the same way as the UNCITRAL Model Law (discussed below). The Conciliation Model Law also deals with fundamental issues in mediation, such as confidentiality, disclosure, admissibility of evidence in other proceedings and enforceability of settlement agreements. Although the Conciliation Model Law has not yet been adopted in Canada, efforts are underway to promote its adoption by the Canadian provinces and the federal government.

---

[9]   See Ontario *Rules of Civil Procedure*, Rule 24.1. One common feature of mediation and arbitration is a concern for confidentiality. See *Rogacki v. Belz* (2003), 67 O.R. (3d) 330 (C.A.) and the discussion in Part XII, below.

At present, certain Canadian arbitration statutes do contemplate mediation during an arbitration proceeding, sometimes permitting the participation of the members of the arbitral tribunal in the mediation without qualification,[10] sometimes permitting their participation only if the parties agree,[11] and sometimes prohibiting that participation.[12] Oddly, the Ontario and Alberta international and domestic arbitration statutes differ from one another in their positions on this issue, while the Québec *Code of Civil Procedure (C.C.P.)*[13] and the *C.C.Q.* are simply silent on this issue.

C. ARBITRATION VERSUS OTHER FORMS OF ADR

Arbitration must also be distinguished from a host of other available mechanisms for alternative dispute resolution ("ADR"). The first of these, med-arb (short-hand for mediation-arbitration), has an arbitration component. Under a med-arb agreement, the parties agree to mediation with the understanding that any issues not settled through mediation will be resolved through arbitration, with the same individual acting as both mediator and arbitrator. A variation on this mechanism is co-med-arb, which uses two individuals to perform the roles of mediator and arbitrator, thereby reducing the possibility in med-arb that parties are reluctant to fully exploit the possibilities of the mediation component of the mechanism.

Another distinct ADR mechanism is the mini-trial, a structured process comprised of two distinct components. Parties engage in an information

---

[10] *Alberta Domestic Act, infra* note 27, s. 35; *Saskatchewan Domestic Act, infra* note 27, s. 35; *Manitoba Domestic Act, infra* note 27, s. 35(2); *Nova Scotia Domestic Act, infra* note 27, s. 39(4).

[11] *British Columbia International Act, infra* note 28, s. 30; *Alberta International Act, infra* note 28, s. 5.

[12] *Ontario Domestic Act, infra* note 27, s. 35.

[13] R.S.Q. c. C-25.

exchange that provides an opportunity to hear the strengths and weaknesses of one's own case as well as the cases of the other parties involved, before turning to negotiation of the matter. In the mini-trial, a representative for each party presents an abbreviated version of that side's case. The case can be heard by a former judge but also by senior business representatives from both sides having full settlement authority. It may be presided over by these representatives with or without a neutral advisor, who can supervise and control the information exchange. Following the presentation, the parties' representatives meet, with or without the neutral advisor, in order to negotiate a settlement. Frequently, the neutral advisor will serve as a mediator during the negotiation phase or be asked to offer an advisory opinion on the potential court outcome, in order to guide the negotiators. Such advisory opinions may be given on an issue-by-issue basis, in order to allow the parties to reach their own overall settlement and to maintain the mediator's facilitative (not adjudicative) role for the balance of the meeting.

Other distinct ADR mechanisms include partnering and the use of an ombudsperson. Occasionally parties might agree to use a series of ADR mechanisms in succession, with the aim of reaching a settlement at the earliest possible step. This is referred to as multi-step ADR. Another possible use of ADR mechanisms is a two track approach, according to which ADR mechanisms are used in conjunction with, and sometimes as a condition precedent to, litigation or arbitration.

D. TYPES OF ARBITRATION

In consensual arbitration, the principal focus of this Guide, the disputing parties choose an independent and impartial individual or a panel of such individuals to hear the dispute and to render a final and binding award. On the other hand, the parties may agree in advance that the neutral advisor's decision will be merely advisory in nature. This is sometimes (if somewhat misleadingly) called "non-binding arbitration" or at times *arbitrage*. An incentive tactic may be used in this type of dispute resolution, such that the parties agree to a penalty to be imposed if one party rejects the neutral advisor's decision, resorts to litigation or arbitration, and in so doing fails to improve its position by a specified amount. Penalties may include the payment of interest and legal costs incurred in the litigation/arbitration.

One form of arbitration that is increasingly popular in resolving commercial disputes is "baseball" or "final-offer" arbitration. Final-offer arbitration is used commonly in some industries and is mandatory under certain Canadian legislation.[14] In this process, each party submits a proposed monetary award to the arbitrator. At the conclusion of the hearing, the arbitrator chooses one of the awards without modification. This approach imposes limits on the arbitrator's discretion and creates an incentive for each party to offer a reasonable proposal, in the hope that it will be accepted by the arbitrator. A related variation of this process is "night baseball" arbitration, which requires the arbitrator to make a decision without the benefit of the parties' proposals and then make the award to the party whose proposal is closest to that of the arbitrator.

In "bounded" or "high-low" arbitration, the parties privately agree, without informing the arbitrator, that the arbitrator's final award will be adjusted to fall within a bounded range. For example, if A seeks CAD 200,000 and B is willing to pay only CAD 70,000, the high-low agreement would provide that if the award is below CAD 70,000 it will be bumped up to that amount and if the award is above CAD 200,000 it will be reduced to that amount. If the award is anywhere within the range, the parties are bound to the arbitrator's award with no adjustment.

---

[14] For instance, *Canada Transportation Act*, S.C. 1996, c. 10, Part IV, s. 161, and *Farm Products Marketing Act Regulations*, R.R.O. 1990, Regulation 414, s. 16.

III. Why Choose Arbitration?

Arbitration is second nature in some industries and for some kinds of disputes. Arbitration is mandatory when using some industry standard contracts and is common in franchise and distribution agreements. Arbitration has long been used to resolve labour relations and international sport disputes. Energy companies are constant and very knowledgeable consumers of commercial arbitration services. Some legislation, such as Alberta's *Natural Gas Marketing Act*, requires arbitration for specialized, industry-specific dispute resolution.[15]

Effective and predictable dispute resolution is a key consideration when negotiating agreements that are critical to a company's business, such as shareholder agreements, fuel or raw material supply agreements and long-term product sales agreements. Where two or more parties are co-owners of a plant, resource or business operation, dispute resolution often becomes a prominent issue due to the financial resources invested and mutual benefit derived from a long-term commercial relationship. Appropriate mediation and arbitration provisions may diffuse, or at least quickly resolve, the disagreements that commonly arise in ongoing commercial relationships.

An agreement to arbitrate should also be seen in the broader context of the commercial agreement, in which the parties allocate and mitigate risks, including the risks of a future dispute. Arbitration may also address a number

---

[15] *Natural Gas Marketing Act*, R.S.A. 2000, c. N-1, s. 13.

of perceived problems for companies that do business in Canada or wish to avoid other jurisdictions whose laws have undesirable features.

Consider the following features of Canadian law and procedure, many of which have emerged or been reaffirmed in the past ten years:

– As in the judicial systems of many countries, Canadian courtrooms are open to the public and the media is free to report on evidence from the proceedings. Court-ordered closing of the courtroom and sealing of the court records are very rare, particularly in commercial matters.[16]

– Like many other jurisdictions, Canada's provincial rules of civil procedure permit very broad oral and documentary discovery, despite some recent efforts to contain their scope.[17]

– Punitive damages are now available in breach of contract cases, without a separate cause of action arising at the time of the breach. The Supreme Court of Canada has recently upheld punitive damages awards of as much as $1 million.[18]

– Canadian law on fiduciary duties is arguably the broadest in the common law world, sometimes extending to a commercial setting. The remedies for breach of fiduciary duty are intrusive and include monetary awards, rescission and disgorgement of profits made by the breaching party.[19]

---

[16] See *MacIntyre v. Nova Scotia (Attorney General)*, [1982] 1 S.C.R. 175; *Dagenais v. Canadian Broadcasting Corp.*, [1994] 3 S.C.R. 835; *Atomic Energy of Canada Ltd. v. Sierra Club of Canada* (2002), 211 D.L.R. (4th) 193 (S.C.C.).

[17] Compare, for example, the Ontario *Rules of Civil Procedure*, Rules 30.03 and 31.06 with the Alberta *Rules of Court*, Rule 186.1, which was adopted (Alta Reg. 172/99) with the intention of narrowing the scope of discovery.

[18] See *Hill v. Church of Scientology of Toronto*, [1995] 2 S.C.R. 1130 (a defamation case); *Whiten v. Pilot Insurance Co.*, [2002] 1 S.C.R. 595; and *Performance Industries Ltd. v. Sylvan Lake Golf & Tennis Club*, [2002] 1 S.C.R. 678.

[19] See *LAC Minerals Ltd. v. International Corona Resources Ltd.*, [1989] 2 S.C.R. 574 (1989), 61 D.L.R. (4th) 14, and generally, J.D. McCamus, "Prometheus Unbound:

– It seems that many courtroom trials involve a battle of experts. The result has been a marked increase in the complexity, expense and length of court proceedings.

– Most Canadian provinces now have class action legislation; several now permit contingency fees for lawyers.[20]

Management of risk in contractual relationships is an increasingly important and complex task, whether the agreement is a standard form consumer agreement or a multi-party agreement with signatories in several countries. There are a number of avenues that parties may choose in order to manage (or allocate) economic risk, enhance certainty, and foster predictability when drafting complex agreements. One aspect of such risk management is a carefully drafted arbitration provision. That is not to say that arbitration does not have inherent virtues, but the choice of arbitration should be a conscious one, keeping in mind the objectives of the parties.

The negotiation of dispute resolution provisions and arbitration clauses in particular raises distinct issues for every agreement. In addition to the broad advantage of flexibility to manage risk, some of the advantages of arbitration over traditional court litigation in commercial matters are:

– ***Privacy.*** Litigation is conducted in a public forum. In commercial matters, anyone can attend court proceedings and examine the court file. Information may be disclosed in the course of litigation that may be confidential, business-sensitive, or embarrassing to the parties. While courts occasionally do seal a court file and restrict access to hearings,

---

Fiduciary Obligation in the Supreme Court of Canada" (1997) 28 Can. Bus. L.J. 107 and the cases cited therein.

[20] Alberta and Manitoba recently joined British Columbia, Saskatchewan, Ontario, Québec and Newfoundland as provinces with class action legislation. See *Class Proceedings Act*, R.S.B.C. 1996, c. 50; *Class Proceedings Act*, S.A. 2003, c. C-16.5; *The Class Proceedings Act*, S.M. 2002, c. 14; *Class Proceedings Act*, 1992, S.O. 1992, c. 6, s. 5; *C.C.P.*, Article 1003; *Class Actions Act*, S.N.L 2001, c. C-18.1.

these protections are not assured and the public interest in an open court system usually trumps the privacy interests of the parties. Privacy and even confidentiality, however, may be lost if parties to an arbitration resort to the courts for interim relief, enforcement, appeal or setting aside (annulment in Québec) assistance.

– ***Choice of Arbitrator.*** Judges come from a variety of backgrounds and have different experiences and expertise. In the court system, one may be assigned a judge who is unfamiliar with complex commercial issues. Unfamiliarity raises the spectre of unpredictability, which in most commercial settings is something to be avoided. Parties to an arbitration agreement, however, may choose their own independent and impartial arbitrator. Not only can parties choose an arbitrator with commercial law experience, if circumstances demand, but they may also choose an arbitrator with industry-specific or technical expertise.

– ***Procedural Flexibility and Speed.*** The civil procedure rules in court can be rigid and may provide a recalcitrant litigant with the means to drag out the proceedings for many years. Arbitration, in contrast, is conducted in private and may be structured by the parties to suit their particular interests and the nature of their commercial relationship. Interlocutory applications are less frequent in an arbitration and the scope of document production and oral discovery, if any at all, is often more restricted than in North American litigation. In addition, decisions are often speedier; once a hearing is completed, the arbitrator(s) may render a decision within weeks, whereas courts may take longer and be subject to appeals of both interlocutory and final orders. Arbitration clauses will often specify a timeframe within which an award must be made by the arbitrator(s) after the completion of a hearing.

– ***Continuity.*** The involvement of the arbitrator(s) from appointment through the pre-hearing to the hearing phase provides a level of continuity that is often lacking in the court system. This continuity makes arbitrations more efficient than litigation where parties are faced with educating each master or judge dealing with pre-trial matters or coping with an inflexible case management schedule. The continuing involvement of the arbitrator(s) in preliminary matters may also dissuade the parties from unnecessary procedural wrangling.

– **Finality.** Arbitration generally offers commercial parties an award that is final and less vulnerable to the delays and uncertainty inherent in the litigation appeal process. As set out below, Canadian arbitration statutes provide narrower grounds upon which an arbitral award may be challenged compared with ordinary litigation appeal procedures.

– **Enforcement.** Domestic arbitration offers little practical advantage over court litigation in terms of enforcement. International arbitration, however, offers substantial and unique advantages over litigation when it comes to enforcement. Canadian court judgments can only be enforced in foreign jurisdictions if there is a reciprocal enforcement treaty in effect or if the successful party sues on the judgment in a foreign court. By contrast, international arbitration awards are enforceable in over 140 countries under the United Nations Convention on the Recognition and Enforcement of Foreign Arbitral Awards (the "New York Convention").

Are arbitrations right in every case and for every party? Not at all. Courts retain a number of important features that may make them preferable to arbitration. There are no charges for judges or court facilities; courts often allow more fulsome appeal rights on the merits, both legal and factual; they accommodate multiple party disputes and the addition of third parties to the proceedings; and they afford full procedural protections to all parties, including wide discovery and quick access to *ex parte* interim relief such as a *Mareva* injunction or *Anton Piller* order. And Canadian Courts in some kinds of commercial matters are increasingly sensitive to concerns such as decision-making in "real-time" and having one judge assigned to manage complex or time-sensitive matters.

What is important is that commercial parties make well-informed decisions with regard to their chosen forum for dispute resolution in order to achieve their business objectives as efficiently as possible.

IV. The Arbitration Landscape in Canada

A. CANADIAN ARBITRATION LEGISLATION AND THE UNCITRAL MODEL LAW

Canada is a federal state comprising ten provinces and three territories. The basis for the division of powers between the provinces' legislatures and the Parliament of Canada is the *Constitution Act, 1867*. While no power is expressly contemplated in the Constitution, commercial arbitration is, except for certain narrow purposes, a matter for the jurisdiction of the provincial legislatures.[21]

In 1985, some Canadian legislators recognized the underdeveloped state of arbitration legislation in Canada. Prior to this time, the federal government had not acceded to the New York Convention, which had been adopted by the United Nations Conference on International Commercial Arbitration in 1958.

Enticed by the opportunities available to Canadian business through the expanding Pacific Rim economies, British Columbia legislators led the effort to sponsor the federal-provincial agreements that allowed the adoption of the New York Convention. In May, 1986 Canada acceded to the New York

---

[21] M. Lalonde, *International Handbook on Commercial Arbitration* (Kluwer Law International), Suppl. 42, November 2004, at 1.

Convention, and the federal government then passed the *United Nations Foreign Arbitral Awards Convention Act*, which made the Convention part of the law of Canada. The provinces followed suit and each passed legislation adopting the New York Convention as part of provincial law.[22]

In addition, the federal government became the first jurisdiction to adopt the UNCITRAL Model Law on international commercial arbitration. The decisive and systematic implementation of the UNCITRAL regime throughout Canada has been described by one American observer as "a beacon to the US and the rest of the world."[23] The provinces again followed, revising their domestic arbitration statutes to conform to the modern approach of the UNCITRAL Model Law.[24]

Central to the philosophy of the UNCITRAL Model Law is the idea of party autonomy. As many decisions now demonstrate, Canadian courts have embraced this principle.[25] The guiding principles of the UNCITRAL Model

---

[22]   *Infra* note 283.

[23]   I.I. Dore, *The UNCITRAL Framework for Arbitration in Contemporary Perspective* (London/Boston: Graham & Trotman/Martinus Nijhoff, 1993) at 183. The *Explanatory note by the UNCITRAL Secretariat on the Model Law on International Commercial Arbitration* describes the UNCITRAL Model Law as "a sound and promising basis for the desired harmonization and improvement of national laws. It covers all stages of the arbitral process from the arbitration agreement to the recognition and enforcement of the arbitral award and reflects a worldwide consensus on the principles and important issues of international arbitration practice."

[24]   *Infra* note 283. As discussed below, the common law provinces generally attached the UNCITRAL Model Law as a schedule to their respective international commercial arbitration legislation. The exception is British Columbia, which drafted its own legislation based on the UNCITRAL Model Law. For its part, Québec's *C.C.P.* requires that the UNCITRAL Model Law be "taken into consideration" in the interpretation of Book VII, Title I.

[25]   *Quintette Coal Ltd. v. Nippon Steel Corp.* (1990), 50 B.C.L.R. (2d) 207 (C.A.), per Gibbs, J.A. at 215-217, leave to appeal to S.C.C. refused (1990), 50 B.C.L.R. (2d) xxviii; *BWV Investments Ltd. v. Saskferco Products Inc.* (1994), 119 D.L.R. (4th) 577 (Sask. C.A.), *per* Gerwing, J.A., at 587-591; *Noble China Inc. v. Lei* (1998), 42 O.R.

Law are as follows:[26]

– parties should be free to design the arbitral process as they see fit, but the arbitral process should be "fair" to both parties;

– parties who enter into valid arbitration agreements should be held to their bargain;

– the arbitration tribunal should be neutral and as unbiased as possible and should be empowered to determine its own jurisdiction;

– the arbitration should proceed in private without substantial intervention by the courts; and

– the resulting award should be readily enforceable, subject only to review for a limited and specified list of significant flaws of form or procedure.

Some of these principles have more importance to parties engaged in international commercial disputes than those involved in domestic disputes. For example, minimum court intervention will often be desirable for international commercial parties who may be reluctant to submit to the jurisdiction of their opponent's courts or that jurisdiction as the place of arbitration. However, in many cases, and as described below, domestic commercial parties may also benefit from the potential advantage of these principles over conventional litigation.

(3d) 69 (Gen. Div.), *per* Lax, J., at 86-94. See also the Supreme Court's analysis of art. 3148 C.C.Q. and its relationship to the UNCITRAL Model Law and the New York Convention in *GreCon Dimter Inc. v. J.R. Normand Inc. et al.* (2005), 255 D.L.R. (4th) 257 (S.C.C.), *per* Lebel, J.

[26] These central features and their primary motivations are canvassed in greater detail in Uniform Law Conference of Canada, *Uniform Arbitration Act, Proceedings of the Seventy-Second Annual Meeting Held August, 1990* (Saint John, New Brunswick) at 88, and E.P. Mendes, "Canada: A New Forum to Develop the Cultural Psychology of International Commercial Arbitration" (1986) 3 J. Int'l Arb. 71.

B. DOMESTIC AND INTERNATIONAL ARBITRATION

In Canada, all nine common law provinces as well as each of the territories have two arbitration statutes: a domestic arbitration statute[27] and an international arbitration statute.[28]

---

[27] B.C: *Commercial Arbitration Act*, R.S.B.C. 1996, c. 55 [*British Columbia Domestic Act*]; Alberta: *Arbitration Act*, R.S.A. 2000, c. A-43 [*Alberta Domestic Act*]; Saskatchewan: *Arbitration Act*, 1992, S.S. 1992, A-24.1 [*Saskatchewan Domestic Act*]; Manitoba: *The Arbitration Act*, 1997, c.4 (C.C.S.M. c. A120) [*Manitoba Domestic Act*]; Ontario: *Arbitration Act*, S.O. 1991, c. 17 [*Ontario Domestic Act*]; New Brunswick: *Arbitration Act*, S.N.B. 1992, c. A-10.1 [*New Brunswick Domestic Act*]; Nova Scotia: *Commercial Arbitration Act*, S.N.S. 1999, c. 5 [*Nova Scotia Domestic Act*]; P.E.I.: *Arbitration Act*, R.S.P.E.I. 1988, c. A-16 [*Prince Edward Island Domestic Act*]; Newfoundland & Labrador: *Arbitration Act*, R.S.N.L. 1990, c. A-14 [*Newfoundland Domestic Act*]; Yukon: *Arbitration Act*, R.S.Y. 2002, c. 8 [*Yukon Domestic Act*]; Northwest Territories & Nunavut: *Arbitration Act*, R.S.N.W.T. 1988, c. A-5 [*Northwest Territories Domestic Act*] [*Domestic Acts* refers to any two or more or all of the Acts herein defined, as the case may be].

[28] B.C.: *International Commercial Arbitration Act*, R.S.B.C. 1996. c. 233 [*British Columbia International Act*]; Alberta: *International Commercial Arbitration Act*, R.S.A. 2000, c. I-5 [*Alberta International Act*]; Saskatchewan: *International Commercial Arbitration Act*, S.S. 1988, c. 1-10.2 [*Saskatchewan International Act*]; Manitoba: *International Commercial Arbitration Act*, S.M. 1986, c. 32 (C.C.S.M. c. C151) [*Manitoba International Act*]; Ontario: *International Commercial Arbitration Act*, R.S.O. 1990, c. I.9 [*Ontario International Act*]; New Brunswick: *International Commercial Arbitration Act*, S.N.B. 1986, c. I-12.2 [*New Brunswick International Act*]; Nova Scotia: *International Commercial Arbitration Act*, R.S.N.S. 1989, c. 234 [*Nova Scotia International Act*]; P.E.I.: *International Commercial Arbitration Act*, R.S.P.E.I. 1988, c. I-5 [*Prince Edward Island International Act*]; Newfoundland & Labrador: *International Commercial Arbitration Act*, R.S.N.L. 1990, c. I-15 [*Newfoundland International Act*]; Yukon: *International Commercial Arbitration Act*, R.S.Y. 2002, c. 123 [*Yukon International Act*]; Northwest Territories & Nunavut: *International Commercial Arbitration Act*, R.S.N.W.T. 1988, c. I-6 [*Northwest Territories International Act*]. [*International Acts* refers to any two or more or all of the Acts herein defined, as the case may be].

In Québec, both types of arbitration are referenced in the *C.C.P.*, which deals with the conduct of arbitration and leaves the procedure of the arbitration and the manner in which evidence is taken during the arbitral process to the parties and the arbitral tribunal. The *C.C.P.* also covers the recognition and enforcement of domestic and foreign arbitral awards. On the other hand, the *C.C.Q.* identifies the criteria for the validity of arbitration agreements and, with the exception of questions of public order and certain matters such as the status of persons,[29] permits parties to submit any dispute to arbitration and for them to define the arbitrator's terms of reference.

Under the provisions of the common law provinces' legislation, the domestic statute is the default statute: it will apply to all arbitrations conducted pursuant to an arbitration agreement in the province, unless the provincial international arbitration statute applies to the arbitration.[30]

There is a separate federal statute for all arbitrations involving the government of Canada, whether domestic or international. The federal statute is based on the UNCITRAL Model Law.

1. "International" Arbitration

All of the provincial international arbitration statutes incorporate and adopt the UNCITRAL Model Law. Article 1(3) of the UNCITRAL Model Law uses three criteria to determine whether an arbitration is "international." First, an arbitration is international if the parties to an arbitration agreement have, at the time of the conclusion of that agreement, their places of business in different

---

[29] See Article 2639 *C.C.Q.* which reads:

> Disputes over the status and capacity of persons, family matters or other matters of public order may not be submitted to arbitration.

> An arbitration agreement may not be opposed on the ground that the rules applicable to settlement of the dispute are in the nature of rules of public order.

[30] *The United Mexican States v. Metalclad Corporation* (2001), 89 B.C.L.R. (3d) 359 (S.C.) at 371.

States. Secondly, an arbitration is international if one of the following places is situated outside the state in which the parties have their places of business:

- the place of arbitration if determined in or pursuant to the arbitration agreement;
- any place where a substantial part of the obligations of the commercial relationship is to be performed or the place with which the subject matter of the dispute is most closely connected.

Thirdly, if the parties have expressly agreed that the subject matter of the arbitration agreement relates to more than one country, the arbitration is considered international.

If a party has more than one place of business, the place of business used for determining whether the arbitration is international is the place that has the closest relationship to the arbitration agreement. If a party does not have a place of business, reference is to be made to his habitual residence.

Each province's international arbitration legislation, however, is not identical. There are differences that influence which of the arbitration statutes will apply to a dispute.

i. *Common Law Provinces*

According to section 1(7) of the *Ontario International Act*, the references to "different States" found in subsections (a) and (b) of Article 1(3) of the UNCITRAL Model Law mean "different countries," and the reference to "States" means "countries." Hence, for the purposes of the *Ontario International Act*, an arbitration between parties who, at the time of the conclusion of the arbitration agreement, had their places of business in two different provinces would be considered domestic and subject to the mandatory sections enumerated in section 3 of the Act.

The *British Columbia International Act* arrives at the same result by declaring that the provinces and territories of Canada are considered "one state."

The *Alberta International Act*, however, is silent as to whether the domestic or international legislation applies to an inter-provincial arbitration.

ii. Québec

Unlike the other Canadian provinces, Book VII of Title I of Québec's *C.C.P.* applies to both domestic and international commercial arbitrations seated in the province. Moreover, unlike its common law counterparts, the *C.C.P.* requires that, "where matters of extra-provincial and international trade are at issue," Title I (Arbitration Proceedings) be interpreted by "taking into consideration" the UNCITRAL Model Law, the Report of UNCITRAL and the Analytical Commentary on the draft text of the UNCITRAL Model Law.[31] No reported court decision in Québec has addressed the issue of what "taking into consideration" the UNCITRAL Model Law means.

iii. Federal

The definition of "international" found in Article 1(3) of the UNCITRAL Model Law also applies to arbitrations governed by the *Commercial Arbitration Act* (the "*Federal Act*").[32] The *Federal Act* applies "only in relation to matters where at least one of the parties to the arbitration is Her Majesty in right of Canada, a departmental corporation or a Crown corporation or in relation to maritime or admiralty matters." The *Federal Act* is silent as to whether the provinces and territories of Canada are considered one state.

C. "COMMERCIAL" ARBITRATIONS

The UNCITRAL Model Law recommends that the term "commercial" be given a broad meaning to cover "matters arising from all relationships of a

---

[31] Article 940.6 *C.C.P.*

[32] R.S.C. 1985, c. 17 (2nd Supp.).

commercial nature, whether contractual or not." According to an explanatory note to the UNCITRAL Model Law:[33]

> [r]elationships of a commercial nature include, but are not limited to, the following transactions: any trade transaction for the supply or exchange of goods or services; distribution agreement; commercial representation or agency; factoring; leasing; construction of works; consulting; engineering; licensing; investment; financing; banking; insurance; exploitation agreement or concession; joint venture and other forms of industrial or business co-operation; carriage of goods or passengers by air, sea, rail or road.

This definition has been adopted in the *British Columbia International Act* to identify those relationships that may be made subject to arbitration.[34] Other provincial statutes enacting the UNCITRAL Model Law and the New York Convention provide less guidance on their application within the context of the statute. In Alberta, Nova Scotia and Newfoundland and Labrador, the relevant *International Act* adopts the language of the New York Convention and applies the New York Convention to awards and arbitration agreements "arising in respect of differences arising out of commercial legal relationships, whether contractual or not." Other provinces' statutes are less specific and simply implement the UNCITRAL Model Law or the New York Convention in respect of "commercial arbitrations" or awards.

The Alberta Court of Appeal has held that the New York Convention and the *Alberta International Act* cover both contractual and non-contractual commercial relationships, including liability in tort, so long as the relationship that creates liability is one that can fairly be described as "commercial." That may include allegations of a conspiracy between a corporation and its subsidiaries. In addition, the Alberta Court of Appeal has held that "commercial" is not to be

---

[33] See Chapter I, Article 1(1), under the heading "Scope of Application."

[34] *British Columbia International Act*, s. 1(6).

equated with "contractual."[35] However, in Alberta, employment relationships are not considered "commercial" under the UNCITRAL Model Law.[36]

The Ontario courts have also interpreted "commercial" broadly. In *Carter v. McLaughlin*, an Ontario court permitted enforcement of a foreign arbitration award for damages arising from the sale of a residential house. The Court concluded that, although the parties involved were not "commercial persons" or merchants, the arbitration was a "commercial" one because the sale transaction was conducted in a business-like manner, with the assistance of professional realtors, "within a legal framework appropriate for a transaction involving a large sum of money." In reaching this conclusion, the court considered an excerpt from the Analytical Commentary contained in the *Report of Secretary General to the Eighteenth Session of UNCITRAL.*[37]

In *United Mexican States v. Metalclad Corp.*, the British Columbia Supreme Court considered an application to set aside an award issued by a North American Free Trade Agreement ("NAFTA") tribunal in an arbitration governed by the ICSID[38] Arbitration (Additional Facility) Rules. Tysoe, J. held that Metalclad had made an investment in a company and the subsequent construction of a landfill facility. Given the applicable section of NAFTA, the court concluded that the relationship between the parties was commercial, not regulatory, in nature.[39]

---

[35] *Kaverit Steel & Crane Ltd. v. Kone Corp.* (1992), 85 Alta. L.R. (2d) 287 at 293 (C.A.). See also *Dunhill Personnel System Inc. v. Dunhill Temps Edmonton Ltd.* (1993), 13 Alta. L.R. (3d) 241 at 244 (Q.B.).

[36] *Borowski v. Heinrich Fiedler Perforiertechnik GmbH* (1994), 29 C.P.C. (3d) 264 (Alta. Q.B.) at 377.

[37] *Carter v. McLaughlin* (1996), 27 O.R. (3d) 792 (Gen. Div.), at 796-798. The *Analytical Commentary* is expressly permitted as a source to aid interpretation of the UNCITRAL Model Law under the *Ontario International Act*, s, 13(b). The subject property in *Carter* sold for CAD 94,000 and the damages awarded were about CAD 12,500.

[38] International Centre for the Settlement of Investment Disputes.

[39] *The United Mexican States v. Metalclad Corporation, supra* note 30 at 372-373.

D. *AD HOC* OR INSTITUTIONAL ARBITRATION

Until recently, *ad hoc* arbitrations were the norm in Canada. These arbitrations do not usually use the services of an arbitral institution to assist in conducting the arbitration process. Rather, the arbitration is governed by the parties' own rules established in their arbitration agreement and any applicable arbitration statutes.

The advantages of *ad hoc* arbitration include potentially lower costs and the parties' ability to shape the arbitral process to meet their requirements and the circumstances of a particular dispute. These potential advantages become even more effective if parties are sufficiently cooperative to design an arbitral process once the dispute arises. Parties can also chose to adopt the UNCITRAL Arbitration Rules which were designed for *ad hoc* arbitration.

Where *ad hoc* procedures are not desired or appropriate, commercial parties may select from a number of arbitral institutions to assist them with the conduct of an arbitration in Canada. These institutions offer administrative services to move the arbitration forward, and, importantly, arbitral appoint-ment procedures in the event that the parties are unable to agree on the sole arbitrator or members of an arbitral tribunal. They also offer well-defined mechanisms for the removal or challenge of arbitrators.

Within Canada, organizations such as the ADR Institute of Canada, Inc., the British Columbia International Commercial Arbitration Centre ("BCICAC") and private companies such as ADR Chambers Inc. and the Osler ADR Centre provide institutional arbitration services. If the parties prefer an institutional arbitration, it is wise to consider using the arbitration clause proposed by the relevant institution and to become familiar with the rules of the institution, many of which are now available on-line.[40]

---

[40] See Appendix; "Codes, rules and model contracts," online: <http://www.iccwbo.org/home/statements_rules/menu_rules.asp>; "Rules and Procedures," online: AAA <http://www.adr.org/RulesProcedures>; "Rules & Protocols," online: ADR Institute of Canada <http://www.adrcanada.ca/rules.html>; "Arbitration Rules," online: ADR Chambers <http://www.adrchambers.com/arbrules.htm>; "Rules of Procedure, Fees

The best known of the international arbitral institutions – including the International Chamber of Commerce ("ICC"), London Court of International Arbitration (the "LCIA") and the American Arbitration Association ("AAA") through its international affiliate, the International Centre for Dispute Resolution ("ICDR") – will provide arbitrators to conduct arbitrations in Canada either in accordance with their own rules of procedure or the UNCITRAL Arbitration Rules. It is noteworthy that Canada is not a signatory to the Washington Convention on the Settlement of Investment Disputes between States and Nationals of Other States which came into force on October 14, 1966 and established the International Centre for the Settlement of Investment Disputes, or "ICSID". Therefore, Canadian companies seeking to agree to arbitrate against a Contracting State over an international investment must use other means, such as the ICSID Arbitration (Additional Facility) Rules or the UNCITRAL Arbitration Rules.

E. ARBITRATION RULES

In an arbitration agreement, parties may agree that their arbitration will be governed by particular arbitration rules offered by a reputable and well-known institution. It is common in international agreements, for instance, for parties to agree to be bound by the rules of arbitration of the ICC, the ICDR, the LCIA, or the Swiss Rules of International Arbitration. Alternatively, parties may wish to design their own rules, or agree to be bound by the UNCITRAL Arbitration Rules, administered by one of the above institutions. In the event that the UNCITRAL Arbitration Rules are chosen, it is important that the parties select an appointing authority, such as one of the institutions identified above, to act as such an authority in the event they cannot, for instance, agree on the identity of the sole arbitrator or Chair of the arbitral tribunal. When

---

and Commencement Forms," online: BCICAC <http://www.bcicac.com/cfm/index.cfm?L=1&P=133>.

using the UNCITRAL Arbitration Rules, parties may also wish to consider using the UNCITRAL Notes on Organizing Arbitral Proceedings.

In the domestic context, if a dispute is governed by the *British Columbia Domestic Act*, the Domestic Arbitration Rules of the BCICAC are applied unless the parties agree otherwise.[41] Similarly, the *Nova Scotia Domestic Act* has a specific schedule attached to the legislation containing procedural rules that will apply to arbitrations, again unless the parties agree otherwise.[42] In Québec, Book VII, Title I of the *C.C.P.* provides the framework for *ad hoc* arbitration. Parties can simply supplement the *C.C.P.* with their own tailor-made rules.

F. JURISDICTION OF THE ARBITRAL TRIBUNAL

Unlike the provincial courts, an arbitral tribunal's principal sources of juris-diction are the arbitration agreement between the parties and any applicable statute.[43] Broadly drafted arbitration provisions, which may incorporate by reference specified arbitration rules, can provide an arbitral tribunal with jurisdiction comparable to a court to decide matters beyond simple contractual issues. Conversely, a narrow agreement may restrict the tribunal's ability to render a comprehensive decision or even preclude arbitration of all or part of a dispute.

---

[41]   *British Columbia Domestic Act*, s. 22 and BCICAC Domestic Commercial Arbitra-tion Rules of Procedure dated as of June 1, 1998 ("BCICAC Domestic Arbitration Rules").

[42]   *Nova Scotia Domestic Act*, s. 33 and Schedule "A."

[43]   *Desputeaux v. Éditions Chouette*, [2003] 1 S.C.R. 178 at paras 22 and 41; *Jardine Lloyd Thompson Canada Inc. v. Western Oil Sands Inc.* (2005) ABQB 509, [2005] A.J. No. 943 (Q.B.), *per* Wittmann, A.C.J., at para 69; *Ontario Hydro v. Denison Mines Ltd*, [1992] O.J. No. 2948.

In the domestic context, an arbitral tribunal's ability to determine its own jurisdiction is recognized by statute, as well as by the rules used by most arbitral institutions. Most provinces' *Domestic Acts* provide that:[44]

> [a]n arbitral tribunal may rule on its own jurisdiction to conduct the arbitration and may, in that connection, rule on objections with respect to the existence or validity of the arbitration agreement.

In British Columbia, there is no such express statutory provision giving the arbitral tribunal the power to determine its own jurisdiction. However, section 22 of the *British Columbia Domestic Act* mandates the application of the BCICAC Domestic Arbitration Rules, unless the parties to an arbitration otherwise agree, and section 20(1) of the BCICAC Domestic Arbitration Rules include the power of an arbitral tribunal to determine its own jurisdiction.

It is clear that the jurisdiction conferred by these provisions on an arbitral tribunal is not exclusive; as a preliminary matter, for instance, the courts may determine whether the arbitral tribunal has jurisdiction to adjudicate, the arbitrability of a dispute, or a constitutional challenge before the tribunal is appointed.[45]

The arbitral tribunal can also decide whether a matter is or is not arbitrable, even in circumstances where one party alleges that the contract is voidable. In this regard, the various *Domestic Acts* provide that the arbitration agreement, even if part of a larger contract, is treated, for the purposes of a ruling on

---

[44] *Alberta Domestic Act*, s. 17(1); *Saskatchewan Domestic Act*, s. 18(1); *Manitoba Domestic Act*, s. 17(1); *Ontario Domestic Act*, s. 17(1); *New Brunswick Domestic Act*, s. 17(1); *Nova Scotia Domestic Act*, s. 19.

[45] *Unifund Assurance Co. v. Insurance Corp. of British Columbia*, [2003] 2 S.C.R. 63 at 84-87; *Ontario First Nations Limited Partnership v. Ontario* (2004), 73 O.R. (3d) 439, 245 D.L.R. (4th) 689 (C.A.) at para. 24 (the arbitral tribunal's jurisdiction is "permissive, rather than exclusive"); *Woolcock v. Bushert et al.*, *infra* note 59 at paras 12-13.

jurisdiction, as an independent agreement that may survive even if the balance of the contract is found to be invalid.[46]

While a statutory right exists in all common law provinces' courts to grant interim relief for the detention, presentation or inspection of property,[47] most provinces also permit tribunals to grant that relief and to issue injunctions and appoint a receiver.[48]

Legislation in Alberta, Saskatchewan, Manitoba, Ontario, New Brunswick and Nova Scotia provides that an arbitral tribunal shall decide a matter in dispute in accordance with law, including equity, and may order specific performance, injunctions and other equitable remedies.[49] British Columbia law expressly permits arbitral tribunals to grant specific performance, and requires that the tribunal adjudicate "by reference to law" unless the parties agree in writing that the matter will be decided on "equitable grounds, grounds of conscience or some other basis."[50] In Québec, Article 944.10 *C.C.P.* permits arbitrators to settle a dispute according to the rules of law that they consider appropriate. They cannot, however, act as *amiable compositeur* without the prior consent of the parties.

In the *International Acts* of the common law provinces, Article 5 of the UNCITRAL Model Law provides that no court shall intervene, except where so provided in the UNCITRAL Model Law. Article 16 provides that the arbitral tribunal may rule on its own jurisdiction including any objections with respect to the existence or validity of the arbitration agreement. Article 16 further

---

[46] *Ontario Domestic Act*, s. 17(2); *Alberta Domestic Act*, s. 17(3); *Saskatchewan Domestic Act*, s. 18(3); *Manitoba Domestic Act*, s. 17(3); *Nova Scotia Domestic Act*, s. 19(3).

[47] See, for instance, *Alberta Domestic Act*, s. 8(1); *Ontario Domestic Act*, s. 8(1). Interim remedies are discussed in Part V, below.

[48] See *Alberta Domestic Act*, ss. 18(1) and 31; *Ontario Domestic Act*, ss. 18 and 31.

[49] *Alberta Domestic Act*, s. 31; *Saskatchewan Domestic Act*, s. 34; *Manitoba Domestic Act*, s. 31; *Ontario Domestic Act*, s. 31; *Nova Scotia Domestic Act*, s. 34; *New Brunswick Domestic Act*, s. 31.

[50] *British Columbia Domestic Act*, s. 23.

provides that the decision by the arbitral tribunal that the contract is null and void "shall not entail *ipso jure* the invalidity of the arbitration clause." Thus under the UNCITRAL Model Law, "there are essentially two elements to this rule: first, that an arbitral tribunal can rule upon its own jurisdiction, and secondly that, for this purpose, the arbitration clause is separate and independent from the terms of the contract containing the transaction between the parties."[51] In Québec, in addition to the Article 16 of the UNCITRAL Model Law referenced in Article 940.6 *C.C.P.*, these two elements are embraced in Article 2642 *C.C.Q.* and Article 943 *C.C.P.*

The ability of an arbitral tribunal to determine its own jurisdiction (occasionally referred to as an arbitral tribunal's "*kompetenz/kompetenz*") is well known in international arbitration and is broadly stated in both international institutional rules and the UNCITRAL Arbitration Rules. For instance, Article 21 of the UNCITRAL Arbitration Rules provides in part:[52]

Article 21

1. The arbitral tribunal shall have the power to rule on objections that it has no jurisdiction, including any objections with respect to the existence or validity of the arbitration clause or of the separate arbitration agreement.

2. The arbitral tribunal shall have the power to determine the existence or the validity of the contract of which an arbitration clause forms a part. For the purposes of [this article], an arbitration clause which forms part of a contract and which provides for arbitration under these Rules shall be treated as an agreement independent of the other terms of the contract. A decision by the arbitral tribunal that

---

[51] Alan Redfern & Martin Hunter, *Law and Practice of International Commercial Arbitration*, 4th edn (London: Sweet and Maxwell, 2004) at 254 [Redfern & Hunter (4th edn)].

[52] *Ibid.* at 252. See also Article 23 of the LCIA Rules of Arbitration.

the contract is null and void shall not entail *ispo jure* the invalidity of the arbitration clause.

V. The Arbitration Agreement

A. THE AGREEMENT

Article 7 of the UNCITRAL Model Law defines an arbitration agreement as:

> an agreement by the parties to submit to arbitration all or certain disputes which have arisen or which may arise between them in respect of a defined legal relationship, whether contractual or not. An arbitration agreement may be in the form of an arbitration clause in a contract or in the form of a separate agreement.

Similar definitions can be found in the domestic and international statutes of the Canadian common law provinces, in the *C.C.Q.*, which contains the substantive law provisions relating to arbitration in Québec, and in the *Federal Act*.

With certain exceptions, including British Columbia, the domestic statutes applicable in the Canadian provinces do not require that the arbitration agreement be in writing.[53] The UNCITRAL Model Law, Article 7(2), however, requires that an arbitration agreement be in writing.

---

[53] *Alberta Domestic Act*, s. 5(1); *Ontario Domestic Act*, s. 5(3); *Manitoba Domestic Act*, s. 5(1); *Saskatchewan Domestic Act*, s. 6(3); *Nova Scotia Domestic Act*, s. 7(1). See *British Columbia Domestic Act*, s. 7(3).

B. TERMS OF REFERENCE

The phrase "Terms of Reference" is borrowed from the ICC Rules of Arbitration, which set out the requirements for what has become a hallmark of ICC International arbitration.[54] As the Terms of Reference will govern the arbitration's scope and often important aspects of its process, significant care should be taken in its drafting. Depending on the terms of the initial arbitration agreement, parties in a Canadian arbitration may also choose to execute formal "Terms of Reference" or "Terms of Submission to Arbitration" for an arbitration.

Special note should be taken of the scope of the issues to be arbitrated as described in the Terms of Reference, particularly if the respondent has raised jurisdictional objections. If there are unresolved concerns that the claimant's issues do not fall within the scope of the original arbitration clause, an agreement to Terms of Reference that alter or expand the scope of the arbitration agreement, will adversely affect the jurisdiction objection.[55]

---

[54] Article 18 of the ICC Rules of Arbitration provides that an arbitral tribunal constituted under the ICC Rules "shall draw up, on the basis and in the light of the parties' most recent submissions," a document setting out, among other things, a summary of the parties' respective claims and relief sought and a list of issues to be determined.

[55] *Saskatchewan Domestic Act*, s. 6(2); *Ontario Domestic Act*, s. 5(2); *New Brunswick Domestic Act*, s. 5(2), which provide that if the parties to an arbitration agreement "make a further agreement in connection with the arbitration, it shall be deemed to be part of the arbitration agreement." The scope of the Terms of Reference will also affect a party's ability to amend its claims during the arbitration.

C. ARBITRABILITY: WHAT KIND OF DISPUTE MAY BE ARBITRATED?

1. Arbitrability of a Dispute

In general, the parties to an arbitration agreement enjoy "virtually unfettered autonomy" to determine which disputes they wish to submit to arbitration, unless there is a specific constitutional or legislative constraint on that autonomy.[56] Parties may, with appropriate language in a written contract, agree to refer their disputes to arbitration even if the courts have been the traditional forum for dispute resolution or where the remedy is statutory in nature.

Canadian courts have been faced with two principal issues relating to arbitrability: first, whether there are any binding rules, such as legislation, that preclude arbitration and require the matter to be resolved in court or another forum; and second, whether the arbitration agreement is drafted to apply to the dispute(s) that have actually arisen between the parties. The issues are distinct, as one relates to the legal concept of "arbitrability" and the other considers the scope of the terms of a specific agreement. Practically speaking, the second question typically arises when a party applies to a court to stay a proceeding in favour of (or in Québec, refer a matter to) arbitration. Accordingly, that issue will be addressed below.[57]

Unless a statute expressly precludes the use of arbitration to resolve disputes (and uses very clear language in doing so), the parties' agreement to submit a matter to arbitration will usually be respected. If the agreement to arbitrate is drafted to cover the dispute, this principle has been applied even in areas of law where the courts have traditionally been the exclusive

---

[56] *Desputeaux, supra* note 43.

[57] The issue also arises (much less often) in applications to set aside or decline to enforce an arbitration award, where it is alleged that the arbitral tribunal made a decision "on matters beyond the scope of the submission to arbitration."

forum for dispute resolution, such as copyright and builders' liens.[58] Similarly, recent appellate cases in both Ontario and Québec have permitted arbitration of disputes involving allegations under the statutory oppression remedy in the provincial *Business Corporations Act*, where the terms of the arbitration agreement cover the dispute in question.[59]

i. Arbitration of Disputes Traditionally Resolved in Court

The broad scope of party autonomy to refer disputes to arbitration was recently confirmed by the Supreme Court of Canada in *Desputeaux*.[60] This case concerned a copyright dispute between the creators of the children's cartoon character Caillou. An arbitrator issued an award recognizing the plaintiff's reproduction rights under a licensing agreement between the parties. The Québec Court of Appeal annulled the award, in part because the *Copyright Act* (Canada) assigned concurrent jurisdiction over copyright matters to the Federal Court of Canada and the provincial superior courts.

The Supreme Court of Canada, in a unanimous decision, overturned the Court of Appeal's decision and applied a wide interpretation of the arbitrator's mandate, which covered all questions having a "connection with the question to be disposed of." The Court held that the terms of the *Copyright Act* were sufficiently general to include arbitration proceedings as an acceptable means of dispute resolution and that, in the absence of express language,

---

[58] See *Desputeaux, supra* note 43 at paras 42 and 46; *Automatic Systems Inc. v. Bracknall Corp.* (1994), 18 O.R. (3d) 257 at 266 (C.A.); *BWV Investments Ltd. v. Saskferco Products Inc., supra* note 25, *per* Gerwing, J.A., at 593-594. See also: *Seneviratne v. Seneviratne* (1998), 159 D.L.R. (4th) 733 (Alta. Q.B.) (divorce).

[59] *Woolcock v. Bushert* (2004), 246 D.L.R. (4th) 139 at para. 33; *Acier Leroux Inc. v. Tremblay*, [2004] Q. J. No. 2206 (Que. C.A.). See also *Kassem v. Secure Distribution Services Inc.* (2004), 43 B.L.R. (3d) 277 (Ont. Sup. Ct.); *Armstrong v. Northern Eyes Inc.* (2000), 48 O.R. (3d) 442 (Div. Ct.), aff'd [2001] O.J. No. 1085 (C.A.); *Deluce Holdings Inc. v. Air Canada* (1992), 12 O.R. (3d) 131 (Gen. Div.).

[60] *Desputeaux, supra* note 43.

the legislation did not exclude arbitration as an alternative means of dispute resolution.

ii. Arbitration of Statutory Oppression Claims

There has been debate in Canada about whether arbitral tribunals may or should have the jurisdiction to decide other statutory remedies. In particular, there are a number of cases concerning the so-called "oppression" remedy found in the provincial and federal *Business Corporations Acts*. The "oppression" remedy permits a court to intervene in a corporation's affairs when the interests of a "complainant" (typically a security holder, director or creditor) have suffered unfair prejudice or oppression or have been unfairly disregarded by the corporation or its directors.[61] If such "oppression" is proven, the court may grant a remedy to rectify the circumstances.

There have been lingering concerns about the arbitrability of oppression claims and the source, if any, of the power to do so. The statutory provisions creating oppression remedies in the Alberta and Ontario *Business Corporations Act* and the *Canada Business Corporations Act* do not expressly confer on arbitral tribunals the jurisdiction to award these remedies. In fact, the statutes confer jurisdiction on the "court," which is a defined term meaning the superior court of the province.[62] At the same time, nothing in the statutes expressly indicates that the court's jurisdiction in this regard is exclusive, thereby depriving arbitral tribunals of such jurisdiction.

In 1992, an Ontario court refused a motion to stay court proceedings to allow arbitration of oppression issues. Without taking a firm position that an oppression claim was inherently arbitrable, the court held that the claim in that case did not fall within the scope of the arbitration agreement in question.[63] In

---

[61] *Canada Business Corporations Act*, R.S.C. 1985, c. C-44 ("CBCA"), s. 241; Alberta *Business Corporations Act*, R.S.A. 2000, c. B-9 ("ABCA"), s. 242; Ontario *Business Corporations Act*, R.S.O. 1990, c. B.16 ("OBCA"), s. 248.

[62] See the definitions of "court" in CBCA, s. 2(1); ABCA, s. 1(m); OBCA, s. 1(1).

[63] *Deluce Holdings Inc. v. Air Canada*, *supra* note 59.

2000, the Ontario courts were faced with an arbitrator's decision, rendered by a former judge, which concluded that the Ontario *Business Corporations Act* reserved the statutory oppression remedy to the courts. The arbitrator decided that he lacked jurisdiction, unless the arbitration agreement expressly conferred jurisdiction on the arbitrator to grant remedies "as if he were exercising the authority of a judge" of the Ontario Superior Court. On a motion in court to require the dispute to be heard in court, a judge at first instance agreed and held that the dispute could not be decided by the arbitrator.

On appeal, the Ontario Divisional Court remitted the dispute back to the arbitrator, on the grounds that the parties had validly chosen arbitration as the mechanism for resolving their disputes over the valuation and redemption of shares held by a departing employee. In the course of his reasons on behalf of Divisional Court, Archie Campbell, J. stated that it is "open to shareholders, by agreement, to choose arbitration as the sole means of resolving their dispute and thus, absent extraordinary circumstances …, to oust the jurisdiction of the court to entertain oppression remedy proceedings." As there were no extraordinary circumstances suggesting that the parties should not be held to their agreement to arbitrate, the Divisional Court stayed the court proceedings in favour of arbitration. However, in concluding that the dispute in question was covered by terms of the arbitration clause, the court did not shed any light on the nature of an arbitrator's power to grant oppression remedies.[64]

In 2004, the Courts of Appeal in both Ontario and Québec concluded that a sufficiently broad arbitration clause will allow for the arbitration of claims for oppression remedies. In *Woolcock v. Bushert*,[65] the Court of Appeal for Ontario examined the wording of the arbitration clause, which provided for the arbitration of any dispute "relating to" the Agreement, and concluded that it was sufficiently broad to encompass all claims, including

---

[64] *Armstrong v. Northern Eyes Inc.*, *supra* note 59.

[65] *Supra* note 59. See also *T.J. Whitty Investments Corp. v. TAGR Management Ltd.* (2004), 47 B.L.R. (3d) 311 (Ont. Sup. Ct.).

those based on statutory oppression. In *Acier Leroux*,[66] the Québec Court of Appeal considered whether the parties' arbitration agreement had the effect of ousting the court's jurisdiction over a minority shareholder's claim for an oppression remedy. Though the court clearly stated that an oppression remedy can properly be the subject of a conventional arbitration agreement between shareholders, it nonetheless found that the arbitration clause in that case did not encompass claims for oppression. A similar conclusion was reached in a subsequent British Columbia case, where the court found that the arbitration clause did not oust the statutory jurisdiction of the court to determine whether alleged oppressive conduct could give rise to a dissolution or winding up of a corporation.[67]

In all of these cases, the analysis is focused on the terms of the arbitration clause itself (and any additional terms which may have been agreed) as the potential source of an arbitrator's jurisdiction to rule on oppression remedies. In light of the Supreme Court's decision in *Desputeaux*, the courts' conclusion that the statutory oppression remedy is arbitrable appears to be sound.[68]

2. Legislation in the Common Law Provinces

The issue of arbitrability is addressed by statute in the common law provinces. Section 7 of the *Ontario* and *Alberta Domestic Acts*, for instance, provides

---

[66] *Supra* note 59.

[67] *Cut & Run Holdings Ltd. v. Booze Bros. Holdings Inc.* (2005), 2 B.L.R. (4th) 14 (B.C.S.C.)

[68] Although the case law has focused on the arbitration clause as the source of an arbitrator's jurisdiction to decide oppression claims, in some cases it may be argued that there is an implied term in the arbitration agreement that the arbitral tribunal may award remedies as if it were exercising the authority of a judge of the superior court. In the absence of language limiting the tribunal's jurisdiction, such an implied term may give business efficacy to the arbitration agreement. Of course, this is subject to certain limitations: for example, because an arbitral tribunal does not have jurisdiction over third parties, it could not award an oppression remedy that affects third party rights.

that the court can stay a court proceeding that pertains to a matter that is properly the subject of an arbitration agreement. However, the court can refuse to stay the court proceeding and instead dispose of the matter itself where the "subject matter of the dispute is not capable of being the subject of arbitration" under the province's law.

What is arbitrable in the common law provinces must be ascertained from case law and from the specific language of the arbitration agreement at issue. Other than the cases interpreting specific terms of a specific arbitration clause, discussed below, there is little case law from which to discern general guidelines on what is "properly" the subject of an arbitration agreement. However, to the extent that provisions like section 7 of the *Ontario* and *Alberta Domestic Acts* seek to exclude matters in dispute "not capable of being the subject of arbitration under Ontario law," the Supreme Court's reasoning in *Desputeaux* in favour of very limited restrictions on arbitrability should apply in the common law provinces. For example, one would expect that matters such as criminal behaviour, to be in the exclusive jurisdiction of the Courts.

3. Legislation in Québec

The Supreme Court in *Desputeaux* rejected the argument that issues relating to copyright ownership fell outside the scope of what is arbitrable. The court did not apply the prohibition contained in Article 2639 *C.C.Q.* against the arbitration of "disputes over the status and capacity of persons, family matters or other matters of public order."

Instead, the Supreme Court held that, in light of clear legislative policy in favour of dispute resolution through arbitration, courts must take a restrictive interpretation of the notion of "public order" in Article 2639. The Court observed that the Québec legislature explicitly mandated such a restrictive interpretation by providing in paragraph 2 of Article 2639 that "an arbitration agreement may not be opposed on the ground that the rules applicable to settlement of the dispute are in the nature of rules of public order." Unless the matter is truly a fundamental issue of public order, arbitrators *can* dispose of questions relating to rules of public order since such questions can validly be the subject matter of arbitration agreements. The court concluded that copyright ownership, though linked to the notion of the author's personality, is better characterized as an economic or commercial issue not to be equated with those issues relating to the status and capacity of persons or family matters referred to in Article 2639.

D. LEGISLATIVE LIMITS ON ARBITRATION

1. Impact of Consumer Protection Legislation

There are now several examples of Canadian provincial legislatures and the courts imposing limits on parties' ability to refer matters to arbitration or to control the arbitration process. In particular, such intervention has occurred in the context of consumer protection and franchise legislation.

Ontario and Alberta now place limits on arbitration agreements in their consumer protection legislation. Ontario's amendments to the *Consumer Protection Act* in 2002 provide that, where a consumer commences a class action in respect of a matter agreed to be arbitrated, a defendant may not rely on the *Arbitration Act*, 1991 to stay the court proceeding in favour of arbitration unless the plaintiff agreed to arbitration *after* the dispute arose.[69]

Alberta's *Fair Trading Act* provides that certain court actions by consumers may not be commenced or maintained if the consumer's cause of action is based upon a matter that the consumer has agreed in writing to submit to arbitration and the arbitration agreement governing the arbitration has been approved by the provincial minister.[70] Relying on this provision, the courts may

---

[69] *Consumer Protection Act 2002*, S.O. 2002, c. 30, Sched. A, s. 8(4).

[70] *Fair Trading Act*, R.S.A. 2000, c. F-2, s. 16.

refuse to stay a court action pending arbitration if the arbitration agreement has not been so approved.[71]

Legislation in Alberta and Ontario also requires arbitrations of franchise disputes to occur within the province, denying national franchisors a common place of arbitration for all disputes with franchisees.[72]

2. Impact of Class Action Legislation

Most Canadian provinces now have legislation governing class actions commenced in the courts.[73] While there are some differences, the legislation permits a court to "certify" a class action where an identifiable class of plaintiffs, led by a representative plaintiff, commences an action that raises a common issue or issues against the defendant(s). For certification in the common law provinces, a class action must also be the "preferable procedure" for resolving the common issues arising in plaintiffs' claims. Each of these characteristics gives rise to an opportunity for the defendant to defeat the proposed certification of the class action.

What happens if a standard form contract provides for arbitration of all disputes and a plaintiff commences a class action in court for breach of the agreement, alleging common issues with a class of consumers affected by the breach? In normal circumstances, the court is required to stay its proceedings in favour of the arbitration in most Canadian provinces, where a party commences a court action contrary to an agreement to arbitrate.[74] But where class action legislation and arbitration legislation are seemingly in competition, the courts are faced with difficult decisions. The policies inherent in the statutes must be analyzed to reach a conclusion.

---

[71] *Ayrton v. PRL Financial (Alta.) Ltd.*, 2004 A.B.Q.B. 787 (Q.B.).

[72] *Arthur Wishart Act (Franchise Disclosure)*, 2000, S.O. 2000, c. 3, s. 10; *Franchises Act*, R.S.A. 2000, c. F23, s. 17.

[73] *Supra* note 20.

[74] See the discussion in Part VI.

Canadian courts are beginning to grapple with how class actions interact with arbitration agreements. While it is too early to discern a definitive trend in the cases, there are three issues that have already been identified. One focus has been on whether arbitration clauses that effectively preclude class actions in court are "unconscionable,"[75] particularly in consumer contracts where there may be an allegation of unequal bargaining power at the time the contract became effective. In the common law provinces, the courts are also beginning to address the impact, under class action legislation, of the presence of an arbitration clause in a standard form agreement on the issue of whether a class action in court is the "preferable procedure" to resolve the claims and whether an application to stay the court action should be dismissed because the agreement to arbitrate is "inoperative" or invalid under commercial arbitration legislation.[76]

This area promises to develop quickly given the underlying competing policy interests of the provincial arbitration and class action statutes. The policy concerns include upholding the parties' bargain and access to justice for small claims. Suppose an agreement requires arbitration and that the amount at issue is small, the issue is common to many counterparties and the costs of the arbitration (including arbitrator costs and exposure to an award of costs in the arbitration) exceed the amount at issue. In the circumstances, the access to justice objective of the class action may be seen to conflict with the arbitration legislation's principle of holding parties to their bargains. The speedier, less expensive and private arbitration agreed by the parties, it is

---

[75] *Huras v. Primerica Financial Services Ltd.* (2000), 13 C.P.C (5th) 114 (Ont. Sup. Ct.), aff''d (2001), 55 O.R. (3d) 449 (C.A.); *Kanitz v. Rogers Cable Inc.* (2002), 58 O.R. (3d) 299 (Sup. Ct.). See also *Union des consommateurs c. Dell Computer Corporation*, [2004] J.Q. No. 155 (C.S.), aff'd [2005] Q.C.C.A. 570.

[76] *MacKinnon v. National Money Mart Co.* (2004), 203 B.C.A.C. 103, 50 B.L.R. (3d) 291 (C.A.). See also *Smith v. National Money Mart Co.* (2005), 8 B.L.R. (4th) 159 (Ont. Sup. Ct.), aff'd [2005] Carswell Ont 4882 (Ont. C.A.).

argued, should yield to the public class action process to ensure the claim is actually adjudicated on its merits.

To some extent, these issues are being addressed in the consumer contract area by legislation.[77] Yet this is a matter for the courts in many circumstances, because neither the provinces' class action legislation nor their arbitration statutes expressly address what to do if the statutes intersect.

For instance, in *Dell Computer Corporation v. Union des consommateurs*,[78] the plaintiff consumer protection agency brought a purported class action after consumers attempted to buy a computer from Dell's internet website when the website contained a pricing error. Dell's website displayed a notice that all sales were subject to the customer agreement or to Dell's standard terms of sale; the standard terms contained an arbitration clause providing that any dispute arising from the online purchase was to be resolved exclusively by arbitration administered by the U.S. National Arbitration Forum (NAF) headquartered in Minneapolis.

Dell moved to dismiss the proposed class action, arguing that the arbitration clause barred court proceedings. A Québec Superior Court judge refused to dismiss the action and granted certification, holding that the arbitration clause was inconsistent with a *C.C.Q.* provision that gives a Québec court jurisdiction to hear an action involving a consumer contract despite any waiver of jurisdiction by the consumer.

The Court of Appeal unanimously dismissed Dell's appeal but disagreed with the reasons of the trial judge. The Court of Appeal found that the NAF's code of procedure provided for the arbitration to be held in Québec, and that any arbitral award could be enforced or annulled in Québec pursuant to the *C.C.P.* However, the Court of Appeal characterized the arbitration clause

---

[77] See *Consumer Protection Act 2002*, S.O. 2002, c. 30, Sched. A, s. 8 and the discussion in the section immediately above. The legislation blunts the impact of decision in *Kanitz, supra* note 71.

[78] [2004] J.Q. No. 155 (S.C.); aff'd on other grounds [2005] QCCA 570; leave to appeal to the Supreme Court is being sought.

as an external contract which, according to the Court, was not adequately brought to the attention of the representative plaintiff. The arbitration clause was therefore null under the *C.C.Q.*

As a matter of principle after *Dell*, therefore, arbitration clauses in consumer contracts could be enforceable in Québec if the terms of arbitration are brought to the consumer's attention when the agreement is made. The court rejected the plaintiff's argument that the arbitration clause was inconsistent with the intent of Québec's *Consumer Protection Act*: the legislature would have had to expressly indicate that consumer disputes could not be arbitrated, and it had not done so. The court also noted that the legislature had recognized the validity of both arbitration and class actions as dispute resolution mechanisms and noted, significantly, that "there was not specific reference to one procedural vehicle having precedence over the other."

The extensive American experience with arbitration clauses and class actions,[79] and the cases arising under the legislation governing both areas, will provide insights for the court challenges to come. There is often a compelling argument that arbitration can offer a preferable procedure for resolving plaintiffs' claims, especially where the individual arbitration agreements allow for consolidation of various arbitrations.[80]

E. ISSUES TO ADDRESS IN AN ARBITRATION AGREEMENT

The principal issue in negotiating an arbitration clause or agreement is the definition of what matters must be arbitrated. While many agreements seek to arbitrate all disputes between the parties, others contemplate different dispute resolution mechanisms depending on the nature of the disagreement. In addition, arbitration agreements arise at two very distinct times: when a

---

[79]   See for instance *Green Tree Financial Corp. v. Bazzle*, 539 U.S. 444 (2003).

[80]   *Kanitz*, *supra* note 75 at para. 55, citing s. 20 of the *Ontario Domestic Act*. See also *Brimner v. Via Rail Canada Inc.* (2000), 47 O.R. (3d) 793 (Div. Ct.).

commercial agreement is entered into in the first place, and when the parties are already in a dispute. In the latter case, each party will inevitably focus on what procedures and technicalities will provide a perceived advantage in the existing conflict. The negotiation of procedures may be difficult as a result.

Where the parties are entering their agreement in the first place, it must be recognized that negotiation of a complicated dispute resolution clause is often not a priority. This is not only because the parties do not immediately foresee disputes. Rather, there are other matters to negotiate and agree upon that are considered more important (and often they are). In these circumstances, adoption of an arbitration clause with a broad scope and well-known arbitration rules is usually the preferred course. Yet there are pitfalls to this approach, as arbitration rules do not always give a party what it needs to successfully prosecute or defend its case, or other protections and risk management provisions that will ultimately make a difference.

Appropriate arbitration clauses are particularly important in long-term agreements, agreements with multiple parties or where specific issues, such as confidentiality protection, are at the forefront. In these cases, a party's broad risk-management and certainty objectives can be met with careful drafting.

The first question is the scope of the arbitration clause – defining what is to be arbitrated. While each negotiation is different, the following are other important issues to consider:

Selection of the Arbitrator(s). The ability of parties to select their adjudicator represents one of the central advantages of arbitration over conventional litigation. However, if the parties have not set out a clear procedure in their arbitration agreement for the selection of the arbitrator(s) and a time limit within which to appoint the arbitrator(s), this issue can lead to months of frustrating delay and litigation.

Number of Arbitrators. In the interest of minimizing costs and delays, many parties will opt for a sole arbitrator. However, it is also common – if the parties cannot agree on one arbitrator – for an agreement to provide that a panel of three will be chosen with each side appointing one arbitrator and the two appointees agreeing upon a third tribunal member. Alternatively, an appointing authority or a court may appoint the arbitrator if the parties cannot agree. Agreement on the number of arbitrators has an obvious effect on the cost of an arbitration, as each member of the tribunal must be paid for his or her time. Further, it is more difficult to schedule hearings or conferences with a three-member panel than with a single arbitrator. However, tribunals with several members, each with different but relevant experience or expertise, may be advantageous to the parties. In international disputes in particular, parties may wish to have an arbitrator selected by them on a panel.

Place or "Seat" of the Arbitration. The location of the arbitration is important for both legal and practical reasons. As a tactical matter, a party negotiating an arbitration agreement may be reluctant to agree to arbitration in the other party's home and vice versa. Often, a mutually convenient independent location is agreed upon or the parties agree that the place of the arbitration shall automatically be determined depending on which party commences the arbitration. However, such a solution must be approached carefully, as it could be costly and very disadvantageous.

Particularly in the case of international or inter-provincial arbitration, the choice of location may have greater significance. The law of the place of the arbitration, or *lex arbitri*, can dramatically affect a party's ability to obtain and later enforce an arbitral award. Issues including interim relief (such as an injunction), disputes over the appointment and jurisdiction of arbitrators, and certain procedural rights may be resolved by local courts under the law of the place or "seat" of arbitration. There may be mandatory provisions of law that the arbitral tribunal must follow. Local law may also govern some aspects of hearing procedure (such as acquiring evidence from third parties) and appeals from interlocutory or procedural orders of an arbitral tribunal, if any. It is very useful, therefore, to have or obtain an understanding of the arbitration law of the proposed place of arbitration prior to choosing that place as the seat of the arbitration.

There may also be a tactical advantage in choosing the location of the arbitration based on the availability of familiar counsel, common language and confidence in the courts of a particular jurisdiction. In international arbitration, proceedings in a country located far away from witnesses or from senior management of a corporate party may be very inconvenient. Arbitration in a jurisdiction with an underdeveloped infrastructure or outdated arbitration legislation can also be problematic in terms of communication, the use of technology during a hearing or in cases where the parties require a court's assistance to advance the arbitration.

Of course, in some cases, the question of where to arbitrate is much more complicated, and the opposite party's jurisdiction may actually be advantageous if, for example, it contains favourable limitations legislation or liability protection for a party breaching a contract. A careful approach involves investigating the advantages of each jurisdiction when the original agreement to arbitrate is negotiated.

Attornment. Given the discussion above, it may be sensible to ensure that both parties attorn to, and have appointed agents for service in the place of the seat. This agreement may solve problems later if, for instance, a party needs speedy interim relief from the courts prior to the constitution of the arbitral tribunal.

Choice of Law. If arbitration is the chosen means to resolve disputes, the parties' choice of law will be very important in ensuring that the ultimate award is enforceable and that the legal system chosen exhibits principles that will uphold the parties' rights and enforce obligations. This is particularly important when entering into an agreement with a non-Canadian party, where the proposed choice of law is the law of a foreign jurisdiction. The choice of a neutral country's laws (such as those of England, France or Switzerland) may be a useful solution in some cases.

When deciding that the substantive law of a Canadian province will apply, it is sensible to review not only the law that may resolve a dispute (both common or case law and statute law), but also the limitations statute and the applicable arbitration statute of the province to see how these laws interact.

Ad Hoc *or Institutional Arbitration.* While there are many factors that may affect this choice, particularly the applicable institutional rules and the expense of the institution, certain significant factors such as experience in a particular field, scrutiny of awards, and availability of trained staff may drive the selection of an institution. For instance, if the opposite party decides to default on an arbitration, some institutional arbitration rules may prove to be more useful in obtaining an ultimately enforceable award.

Discovery. There is typically no automatic right to oral discovery of the opposite party in an arbitration and documentary discovery may be limited. Although some legislation and some rules contemplate applications to the arbitral tribunal for discovery, in most cases it is sensible to provide expressly for discovery rights, if such rights are in fact desired, even if the extent of those rights are ultimately decided by the arbitral tribunal.

Confidentiality Protection. Confidentiality is often a critical reason for the use of arbitration instead of the courts. Yet it may be surprising that, while arbitrations are clearly *private*, they are not necessarily *confidential*. There are many ways that an unwary party may not be covered by confidentiality protections (for example, if disclosure is required by securities laws) or may lose the benefit of confidentiality protection (for instance, through an appeal if an appeal is permitted under the applicable legislation or setting aside proceedings filed in court).

If the matter involves trade secrets, has potential for adverse media coverage, has possible significance beyond the immediate dispute between the parties (such as a franchise dispute), or is otherwise commercially sensitive, a carefully drafted confidentiality clause is a necessary precaution. The following are some issues that arise in relation to confidentiality and privacy and that may be appropriate to address in an arbitration agreement:

- what to disclose publicly at the commencement of the arbitration;

- whether and how to comment on interim orders from the arbitrator;

- whether and how to report and comment upon the final award;

- how to protect trade secrets (for instance, the location of a mining discovery, a chemical formulae or a recipe, or an industrial process);

– how to protect competitively sensitive information, such as pricing or the cost of production;

– how to exclude competitors from hearing strategic business practices or organizational information;

– how to minimize adverse publicity relating to a dispute; and

– on occasion, how to prevent employees from having to testify in the media glare.

Remedies. In some cases it may be important to specify that the arbitral tribunal has jurisdiction to grant certain remedies, such as specific performance and injunctions, which in litigation are granted in equity. It should be noted that Canadian common law provinces have not in the past shown familiarity with the concepts of *ex aequo et bono* or *amiable compositeur*, although the UNCITRAL Model Law recognizes such a possibility.

Continued Performance Pending the Arbitration Hearing. Terms requiring the parties to continue performance of the agreement pending the decision of the arbitral tribunal (sometimes known as "status quo clauses") are sometimes found in long-term agreements, such as distributorships and commodity purchase and sale agreements. Where a dispute may terminate such a relationship, both sides in these circumstances may wish to consider language compelling continued performance pending a decision from an arbitral tribunal on its merits.

Limitations on Liability and Damages that may be Awarded. Canadian courts have shown a willingness to enforce contractual allocations of risk, specifically in exclusion of liability or limitation of liability situations. Such clauses, which may limit the nature of liability and the amount of damages that may be awarded in a breach of contract or tort proceeding, may also attempt to exclude certain kinds of damages such as punitive damages. Recent court decisions permitting punitive damages to be awarded in breach of contract cases suggest that this kind of clause is increasingly important.

In an arbitration proceeding, such allocation of risk clauses arguably affect not only the parties' mutual obligations but also the jurisdiction of the arbitral tribunal to make an award. These clauses, therefore, may be a significant risk management tool in commercial agreements.

Rights of Appeal. Appeal rights are critical issues for consideration at the stage of negotiating an agreement. In Alberta, Saskatchewan, Manitoba, Ontario and New Brunswick, if the parties have so agreed in writing, they are entitled to bring an appeal with respect to a question of law, a question of fact, or a question of mixed law and fact. Absent an express agreement, a party may appeal on questions of law only after obtaining leave of the court. In Québec, the *C.C.P.* specifically states that the only recourse against an award is an application for its annulment.

For their part, Canadian international arbitration statutes do not contemplate or provide for appeals. Finally, as set out below, it may also be worth considering the use of a private appeal panel, which operates effectively as a second stage in the arbitration.

Finality or Privative Clauses. Parties to domestic arbitration agreements may be well-advised to agree that an arbitral tribunal's award is final and binding and that no appeal from the award is permitted. Finality clauses come in numerous forms and are also known as privative clauses. A strong, carefully drafted privative clause may preclude or severely limit a party's chances of success on appeal.

Costs and Expenses of the Arbitration. Despite their reputation, corporate and commercial arbitrations are often not less expensive than conventional litigation. The common term in commercial agreements providing that each side shall bear its own costs may therefore be an undesirable departure from the ordinary practice of Canadian courts (and under some arbitration rules) of ordering that the unsuccessful party pay some or most of the successful party's legal costs and disbursements. The absence of a potential adverse costs award removes an incentive to settle and fails to deter uncooperative behaviour in the arbitration process.

Mandatory Mediation. Most clauses that impose mediation, or even negotiation and then mediation, prior to arbitration will likely be upheld in Canadian courts if the clauses impose conditions precedent. However, if both sides do not act in good faith and show a *bona fide* interest in resolving the dispute, these pre-conditions to commencing an arbitration may serve simply to delay the proceedings.

Joinder or Consolidation of Arbitrations. Where there are multiple parties, or multiple related agreements with some common parties, it may well be sensible to draft specific mechanisms to achieve the potential costs savings associated with joining or consolidating related arbitrations. An agreement may not only reduce costs, but may also avoid inconsistent awards and permit arbitrators who become familiar with a project, facility or the complexities of a commercial relationship, to adjudicate more effectively.

VI. Commencing an Arbitration

This section addresses a number of issues that are central to getting to arbitration: appointing the arbitral tribunal, enforcing an agreement to arbitrate and obtaining a stay of court proceedings pending the outcome of the arbitration, or dismissing a court action in the presence of an arbitration clause. Before turning to these issues, a technical but important threshold issue must be addressed: how to "commence" the arbitration.

A. TECHNICAL REQUIREMENTS TO COMMENCE AN ARBITRATION

Most of the provincial *Domestic Acts*, including those of Alberta and Ontario, provide that an arbitration may be commenced "in any way recognized by law." Although no rules are prescribed for commencing the arbitration, three methods are expressly recognized: service of a notice on the other party demanding arbitration under the arbitration agreement; service of a notice on the other party to appoint or to participate in the appointment of an arbitrator under the agreement; asking a person who has the power to appoint an arbitrator under the agreement to do so and sending a copy of that request to the other party.[81]

---

[81] *Alberta Domestic Act*, s. 23; *Saskatchewan Domestic Act*, s. 24; *Manitoba Domestic Act*, s. 23; *Ontario Domestic Act*, s. 23; *Nova Scotia Domestic Act*, s. 25.

For the specifics on commencing the arbitration, one must look to the terms of the agreement to arbitrate and to the applicable rules of arbitration (if any) for guidance. Sometimes, a letter referring a specified matter to arbitration will suffice. In other cases, the applicable arbitration rules will have detailed requirements for what must be contained in a notice to arbitrate and how that document must be served on the responding party. The UNCITRAL Arbitration Rules, the BCICAC rules and the ICC Rules of Arbitration,[82] for instance, require the claimant to include certain details about the parties, the arbitration process (such as the identity of the party's nominated arbitrator) and the nature of the claim and relief sought in the arbitration.

In each case it is important to ensure that the applicable procedures, rules and contractual requirements are followed, both for what must be included in a notice to arbitrate and for the technical requirements of delivery to the respondent and to any arbitration institution that may be involved. These technicalities may be quite important, not only for delineating the issues and establishing the jurisdiction of the arbitral tribunal, but also for ensuring that the arbitration is commenced before the expiry of the applicable limitation period. Thus, careful thought should be given to compliance with applicable rules and to what is included in a written notice to arbitrate.

B. APPOINTMENT AND COMPOSITION OF THE ARBITRAL TRIBUNAL

1. Number of Arbitrators

Wherever possible, the parties should try to agree in advance on the number of arbitrators by whom they wish to have their dispute(s) resolved. Some of

---

[82] UNCITRAL Rules of Arbitration, Article 3(3); BCICAC Domestic Arbitration Rules, Rules 8 and 9 and BCICAC International Arbitration Rules, Article 17(3); ICC Rules of Arbitration, Article 4(3).

the factors that ought to be considered in deciding whether to choose a single arbitrator or a panel of three arbitrators include:

- the monetary value of the agreement or transaction;

- the delay inherent in scheduling hearings with three rather than one arbitrator;

- whether or not the dispute includes international and/or extra-provincial issues; and

- the increased cost associated with using three arbitrators rather than one.

Having said this, as the number of arbitrators that will resolve a dispute is an important factor in the dispute resolution process, the domestic and international arbitration statutes of all Canadian provinces have specific provisions addressing this issue.

i. *Common Law Provinces*

Most *Domestic Acts* in the common law provinces provide that if the arbitration agreement does not specify the number of arbitrators who are to form the arbitral tribunal, it shall be composed of one arbitrator. Hence, if parties wish to have a panel of three arbitrators, they should state this explicitly in the arbitration agreement. The situation under the *International Acts*, however, is different; those statutes incorporate the UNCITRAL Model Law, which provides in Article 10 that the default number of arbitrators is three.

ii. *Québec*

Article 941 *C.C.P.* sets out a default rule of three arbitrators when parties to an arbitration agreement stipulate that the proceedings shall take place in Québec pursuant to the *C.C.P.* Under this Article, each party is required to appoint one arbitrator and the two so appointed shall appoint the third. Similarly, in international and extra-provincial arbitrations that are seated in Québec,

Article 10 of the UNCITRAL Model Law, which by virtue of Article 940.6 of the *C.C.P.* ought to be taken into consideration, states that the parties are at liberty to determine the number of arbitrators, failing which the number shall be three. Given this default rule, if the parties wish to have their disputes heard by a single arbitrator, they ought to so stipulate.

iii. Federal

The default rule under the *Federal Act* is three arbitrators for both domestic and international commercial arbitrations. The parties may, however, provide for a different number of arbitrators if they prefer.[83]

2. Appointment of Arbitrators

The mechanism of and time limits for the appointment of arbitrators is one of the most important issues to be considered at the drafting stage of an arbitration clause. What the parties decide or omit to consider while their relationship and commercial dealings remain friendly may end up helping or hurting them when a dispute arises. In such a situation, because the constitution of the arbitral tribunal is integral to the commencement of arbitral proceedings, all arbitration statutes have default provisions controlling the appointment process.

i. Common Law Provinces

The provinces' *Domestic Acts* permit the superior court of the province to appoint an arbitral tribunal composed of one or more arbitrators on a party's application where the arbitration agreement provides no procedure for appointing the arbitral tribunal or if a party has failed to do so within certain time limits. The ability to apply to the court to appoint an arbitrator provides the claimant in an arbitration the greatest flexibility – the claimant can either

---

[83] *Supra* note 32 at s. 10.

agree with the opposing party to a solution to the appointment issue in the number of days acceptable to it or it can turn to court for an appointment. While most of the *Domestic Acts* do not set out a time period for an appointment application to the courts, in international arbitrations, the UNCITRAL Model Law provides for, a 30-day time limit where there is a default in respect of the appointment of an arbitral panel.[84]

ii. Québec

Article 941.1 of the *C.C.P.* gives parties who have expressly or by default agreed to a panel of three arbitrators, and who have not contractually decided on the number of days it ought to take each of them to appoint a party-nominated arbitrator, 30 days "after having been notified by the other party to do so" to appoint an arbitrator, failing which the appointment shall be made by a judge of the Québec Superior Court "on the motion of one of the parties." The identical mechanism is applicable if the two arbitrators appointed by the parties "fail to concur on the choice of the third arbitrator." By virtue of Article 940 *C.C.P.*, parties may vary the 30-day time limit. The appropriate time for appointment is something that ought to be considered at the time of drafting the arbitration clause. The same rules apply if matters of extra-provincial or international trade are at issue, which require the court to take into consideration the UNCITRAL Model Law.

Where the parties have agreed to a single arbitrator and if the procedure for appointment contained in the arbitration agreement proves difficult to put into practice, Article 941.2 of the *C.C.P.* permits a judge "on the motion of one of the parties [to] take any necessary measure to bring about the appointment." This recourse is exactly the same under the UNCITRAL Model Law. The decision of a judge under Articles 941.1 and 941.2 is not subject to appeal. This last provision cannot be waived by the parties.

---

[84]   Article 11(3).

iii. Federal

The situation under the *Federal Act* is the same as that under the UNCITRAL Model Law. Note, however, that requests made under the *Federal Act* can, pursuant to section 6, be made either to the Federal Court of Canada or "any superior, county or district court, except where the context otherwise requires."

3. Selecting an Arbitrator

If the parties to an *ad hoc* arbitration have not agreed on a procedure for the appointment of an arbitrator and are otherwise unable to agree on who should act as arbitrator, arbitration statutes in Canada provide the courts with the power to appoint the arbitrator. However, these statutes do not set out factors to be considered by the court in appointing an arbitrator or arbitral tribunal. The only explicit statutory criteria are that the arbitrator must be independent of the parties and must act impartially. Arbitration provisions in commercial agreements often contain general, or sometimes specific, language requiring that the arbitrator have education or expertise in a particular area.

Parties generally only have resort to the court appointing power under the relevant arbitration statutes when they are unable to reach consensus on the choice of arbitrator or, more often, where one party has refused to acknowledge the validity of the arbitration agreement and therefore has refused to consent to the choice of an arbitrator. In these instances, the appointment of an arbitrator is often resolved by the court as a subsidiary issue. Rightly or wrongly, courts have tended to appoint the arbitrator suggested by the party who successfully argues that the arbitration agreement is valid and the dispute should proceed to arbitration.

The courts in Canada have spent little time canvassing the criteria for selecting an arbitrator. This may be attributed to the fact that parties generally submit the names of qualified candidates. However, courts are attuned to the issue of qualification and will consider the subject matter of the dispute in appointing an arbitrator.[85]

What characteristics are desirable in an arbitrator? In general terms, the satisfaction level of clients and counsel with an arbitration hearing is determined by the same set of factors that lead to satisfaction with a conventional trial. As a result, the most sought-after commercial arbitrators in Canada tend to be those with a reputation for delivering fair, balanced, timely, unbiased and considered awards.

In order to collect reliable information on potential arbitrators, it is wise to conduct electronic legal database searches on the proposed arbitrators' names. These will produce cases in which the potential arbitrators have appeared as counsel or presided as judges. In addition, these searches can sometimes provide information on arbitral decisions that have been reviewed by the courts, which sometimes yields helpful background information on the potential arbitrators' conduct of prior proceedings. A more recent trend in Canada (already common practice in the US and Europe in the context of international arbitration) is to interview potential arbitrators to assess their qualifications and availability to hear the matters in dispute.

4. Use of Private Appointing Authorities

In arbitrations under Canadian statutes or in *ad hoc* international arbitrations, parties may agree that an appointing authority, rather than the local courts, shall make the necessary appointment. Selecting an appointing authority to make appointments for the parties has two advantages. First, if a reputable institution or organization whose main business is the provision of dispute resolution services is chosen, then parties may find themselves less surprised with the appointment than if it was done by a court. Secondly, the time and the fee that appointing authorities will charge for making an appointment will usually be much less than what it would take for the parties to go to court.

---

[85] *Canadian Reinsurance Co. v. Lloyd's Syndicate PUM 91* (1995), 17 C.C.L.I. (3d) 165 (Ont. Gen. Div.).

The potential disadvantage is that appointing authorities will usually limit their appointments to arbitrators on their rosters, or individuals well known to them. In Canada, the ADR Institute and ADR Chambers will act as appointing authorities. In the international context, some of the better known appointing authorities include the ICC, the LCIA and the ICDR. Under the UNCITRAL Arbitration Rules, if no appointing authority has been agreed upon by the parties, or if the appointing authority agreed upon refuses to act or fails to appoint an arbitrator within 60 days of the receipt of a party's request in that regard, either party may request the Secretary-General of the Permanent Court of Arbitration at The Hague to designate an appointing authority.[86]

5. Independence and Impartiality of Arbitrators

The impartiality and independence of adjudicative tribunals is a well-established hallmark of natural justice in Canada. Where a reasonably well-informed observer would identify a reasonable apprehension of bias based on the lack of impartiality or independence of a member of the arbitral tribunal, that member will be disqualified from serving on the tribunal. If an award has been rendered and a party subsequently becomes aware of a lack of impartiality or independence, the award may be set aside.[87]

In 1955, years before the passage of the modern statutes that govern arbitrations, the Supreme Court of Canada in *Szilard v. Szasz* explained the importance of independence and impartiality in an arbitration:

> [f]rom its inception arbitration has been held to be of the nature of judicial determination and to entail incidents appropriate to that fact. The arbitrators are to exercise their function not as the advocates of the parties nominating them, and a fortiori of one party when they are agreed upon by all, but with as free, independent and impartial minds as the circumstances permit. In particular they must be

---

[86]   Articles 6(2) and 7(2)(b) of the UNCITRAL Arbitration Rules.

[87]   *Alberta Domestic Act*, s. 45(1)(h); *Ontario Domestic Act*, s. 46(1)8.

untrammelled by such influences as to a fair-minded person would raise a reasonable doubt of that impersonal attitude which each party is entitled to.[88]

The court concluded that a "probability or reasoned suspicion" of a biased appraisal and judgment, even if unintended, will defeat the entitlement to an impartial and independent adjudication. Each party, the court reasoned, is entitled to "sustained confidence in the independence of mind of those who are to sit in judgment" in the arbitration.[89]

Since that decision, while there has been international debate as to whether these characteristics are required for a fair hearing,[90] many Canadian cases have upheld the need for impartiality and independence of courts and adjudicative tribunals.[91] Only when the parties expressly provide in their agreement that a member of a tribunal is not to be independent (for instance, if the agreement provides that one member will represent one party or another on the tribunal), will the requirement for an impartial and independent tribunal be relaxed.[92]

i. Common Law Provinces

The *Ontario* and *Alberta Domestic Acts* require that an arbitrator be independent of the parties and act impartially. Hence, before accepting a mandate, an arbitrator must disclose to all parties to the arbitration, any circumstances of

---

[88]   [1955] S.C.R. 3 at 4.

[89]   *Ibid.* at 7.

[90]   Redfern & Hunter (4th edn), *supra* note 51 at 199-206.

[91]   *Committee for Justice and Liberty v. National Energy Board* (1976), [1978] 1 S.C.R. 369 at 391; *Newfoundland Telephone Co. v. Newfoundland (Board of Commissioners of Public Utilities)*, [1992] 1 S.C.R. 623.

[92]   See, for instance, *Terrace Bottle Depot v. Encorp Pacific (Canada)*, [2004] B.C.J. No. 2391 (C.A.) at paras 34ff.

which he or she is aware that may give rise to a reasonable apprehension of bias.

For international arbitrations, Article 12 of the UNCITRAL Model Law requires any person who is approached to be an arbitrator in an international commercial arbitration to disclose any circumstances likely to give rise to justifiable doubts as to his impartiality or independence. While in the past, a distinction had been drawn between "impartiality" and "independence," there appears to be a distinct trend towards viewing these two concepts as the opposite side of the same coin and to use them as parallel tools for assessing the potential for actual or apparent bias.[93]

ii. Québec

The *C.C.P.* is silent on questions of independence and impartiality. However, Article 2641 of the *C.C.Q.* renders null any stipulation that "places one party in a privileged position with respect to the designation of the arbitrators."[94]

iii. Federal

Arbitrators appointed under the *Federal Act* are subject to the same duties as those set out in Article 12 of the UNCITRAL Model Law.

6. Challenging an Arbitrator's Appointment

i. Common Law Provinces

Canada's arbitration statutes and most institutional arbitral rules provide that a party may challenge the appointment of an arbitrator. The grounds for such

---

[93]   Redfern & Hunter (4th edn), *supra* note 51 at 201.

[94]   *Desbois v. Industries A.C. Davie Inc.*, 200-09-000700-879, J.E. 90-994 (26 April 1990) (C.A.Q.). The term "designation" has been interpreted to mean more than just "appointment to or selection of a person for an office or service:" Webster's New Collegiate Dictionary (1981), *s.v.* "designation."

an application are related to impartiality and qualifications. The *Domestic Acts* provide that a party may challenge an arbitrator only on one of the following grounds: [95]

- circumstances exist that may give rise to a reasonable apprehension of bias; or
- the arbitrator does not possess qualifications that the parties have agreed are necessary.

The UNCITRAL Model Law provides that an arbitrator may be challenged if there are "justifiable doubts as to the arbitrator's impartiality or independence."

Many cases provide examples of reasonable apprehension of bias, such as meeting with one of the parties before the arbitration to discuss strategy and tactics; making statements or expressing opinions which indicate that the arbitrator is acting as a proponent of the party who appointed the arbitrator; or, where the arbitrator is made aware of information prejudicial to one party which might otherwise not be admissible in the arbitration.

A party who wishes to challenge an arbitrator must send the arbitral tribunal a statement of the grounds for the challenge within 15 days of becoming aware of these grounds.[96] The arbitrator can then resign or the parties can agree to have the challenged arbitrator removed (whereupon the arbitrator's mandate terminates). Failing resignation or agreement of the parties to remove the arbitrator, the arbitral tribunal rules on the matter and notifies the parties of its decision. If the arbitral tribunal rejects the challenge, the challenging party

---

[95] Section 15(1) of the *Domestic Acts* of Alberta, Manitoba, Ontario and New Brunswick; *Saskatchewan Domestic Act*, s. 16(1); *Nova Scotia Domestic Act*, s. 17(1). See also section 18(1) of the *British Columbia Domestic Act*.

[96] *Alberta Domestic Act*, s. 13(3); *Ontario Domestic Act*, s. 13(3); UNCITRAL Model Law, Article 13(2), Article 942.3 *C.C.P.*

is then entitled to apply to the court to decide the challenge.[97]

ii. Québec

Under the *C.C.P.*, an arbitrator can be recused on the same grounds as a judge. These grounds are enumerated in Articles 234 and 235, to which the *C.C.P.* adds one additional ground solely applicable to arbitrators: the arbitrator lacks the qualifications agreed to by the parties.[98] The grounds for recusal listed in Articles 234 and 235 encompass the following situations:

– the arbitrator is related to one of the parties by blood or marriage or connected to a party as a legal representative, administrator of property, successor, donee, or member of a legal person;

– the arbitrator is himself a party to a similar dispute;

– the arbitrator has given advice on the matter, has taken cognizance of the matter as an arbitrator or has acted as counsel for any party;

– the arbitrator has made known his opinion extra-judicially;

– the arbitrator is interested in a matter which one of the parties will judge;

– the arbitrator has a relationship of entity with one of the parties; or

– the arbitrator has any interest in favouring one of the parties.

Article 234, paragraph 10 of the *C.C.P.* provides another broad ground for recusal: that "there is reasonable cause to fear that the [arbitrator] will not be impartial." All those grounds enumerated above constitute situations that would give rise to a "reasonable apprehension of bias," such that the *C.C.P.*

---

[97] Section 13(6) of the *Ontario* and *Alberta Domestic Acts* provide ten days for application to the Court whereas Article 13(3) of the UNCITRAL Model Law provides the parties with 30 days to bring the court application.

[98] Article 942 *C.C.P.*

effectively employs the same test. The additional ground of reasonable fear of partiality in the *C.C.P.* suggests that, if anything, the test in Québec is even broader than that in Ontario.

The procedural steps for the recusal of an arbitrator are set out in Article 942.2 and following of the *C.C.P.* The party proposing recusal must send a written statement of reasons to the arbitrators within 15 days of becoming aware of the appointment of all the arbitrators or a ground of recusal.[99] The appointing party may only propose recusal on a ground that has arisen or been discovered since appointment.[100] If the arbitrator in question does not withdraw, the matter is decided by the other arbitrators[101] or, if necessary, a judge.[102]

The *C.C.P.* also provides for the revocation of an arbitrator's appointment where he is unable to perform his duties or fails to perform them in a reasonable time.[103]

7. Corporations as Arbitrators?

Parties should consider whether the applicable statute at the seat of the arbitration permits corporations or other legal entities, such as partnerships, to act as arbitrators when drafting arbitration clauses. According to the Supreme Court of Canada in *Sport Maska Inc. v. Zittrer*,[104] where there is no express stipulation by the parties, this issue will be determined by the applicable law where the arbitration is taking place. In Québec, Article 942 *C.C.P.* makes it clear that only a natural person can act as an arbitrator. Provisions in common law provinces such as section 14 of the *Ontario* and *Alberta Domestic Acts*,

---

[99]   Article 942.3 *C.C.P.*

[100]   Article 942.2 *C.C.P.*

[101]   Article 942.3 *C.C.P.*

[102]   Article 942.4 *C.C.P.*

[103]   Article 942.5 *C.C.P.*

[104]   *Supra* note 6 at para. 124.

which provide that an arbitrator's mandate is terminated when the arbitrator resigns or dies, may implicitly preclude anyone other than a natural person from acting as an arbitrator. The UNCITRAL Model Law, on the other hand, contains no such provision.

VII. Enforcing an Agreement to Arbitrate

All of the provinces' *Domestic Acts* and the UNCITRAL Model Law recognize that the courts must be involved in enforcing an agreement to arbitrate. Where parties have agreed to resolve a dispute by arbitration, the courts have long been entitled to ensure that the parties abide by their bargain.[105]

Today, the remedy is a stay of proceedings or a reference to arbitration when a party commences a court action in the face of an arbitration agreement. In addition, the court has jurisdiction in rare cases to stay an arbitration, pending the disposition of a court proceeding.

A. STAYS AND REFERRALS TO ARBITRATION OF COURT PROCEEDINGS

1. Stays or Referral to Arbitration under the *Domestic Acts*

i. The Legislation and its Underlying Policy

The "very strong" legislative policy of the Canadian provinces is to support the arbitration process by holding parties to their agreement to arbitrate

---

[105] See *Arbitration Act*, 1697, 9 William III, c. 15, discussed in *Stancroft Trust Ltd. et al. v. Can-Asia Capital Co.* (1990), 43 B.C.L.R. (2d) 341, 67 D.L.R. (4th) 131 (C.A.).

disputes.[106] In that context, it will not be surprising that, where an agreement requires that a dispute be resolved by arbitration but one party commences a proceeding in court, the responding party may commence an application to stay the court proceeding. Under the *Domestic Acts* of most provinces, including Ontario and Alberta, the court is *required* to stay the proceeding, or, in Québec, to refer the parties to arbitration.[107] In other Canadian jurisdictions, the courts retain discretion to refuse a stay of proceedings.[108]

At least one Court of Appeal has held that, by requiring court proceedings to be stayed in favour of arbitration, modern Canadian arbitration legislation has eliminated the distinction between ordinary arbitration clauses and the traditional *Scott v. Avery* clauses.[109] Thus, where the language of the legislation is mandatory, the parties need not formally agree that arbitration is a condition precedent to litigation to ensure their arbitration agreement is respected.[110]

Mr. Justice Blair in *Deluce Holdings v. Air Canada* described the policy of the Ontario legislation:

---

[106] See, for instance, *Boart Sweden AB et al. v. NYA Stromnes AB et al.* (1988), 41 B.L.R. 295 (Ont. Gen. Div.) at 303; see also *Armstrong v. Northern Eyes, Inc.* (2000), *supra* note 59, and *Prince George (City) v. McElhanney Engineering Services Ltd* (1995), 9 B.C.L.R. (3d) 368 (C.A.).

[107] *Babcock and Wilcock Canada Ltd. v. Agrium Inc.*, *supra* note 1 at 107 (para 7) (noting the "distinct change in policy" from the previous permissive legislation); *New Era Nutrition v. Balance Bar* (2004), 357 A.R. 184, at 193, 245 D.L.R. (4th) 107, *per* Conrad, J.A., at para. 36 (C.A.); *International Resource Management (Canada) Ltd. v. Kappa Energy (Yemen) Inc.* (2001), 281 A.R. 373 (C.A.).

[108] Namely, Newfoundland and Labrador, Prince Edward Island, Yukon and Northwest Territories.

[109] *Scott v. Avery* (1856), 10 All E.R. 1121 (H.L.).

[110] *Babcock and Wilcock Canada Ltd. v. Agrium Inc.*, *supra* note 1. The Court noted at 107, para. 11 that the right to arbitration was "extinguished through the expiration of the limitations period."

The *Arbitration Act, 1991* imposes what is tantamount to a mandatory stay of court proceedings, with certain limited exceptions, in
circumstances where the parties have agreed to submit their dispute
to arbitration. This legislation represents a shift in policy towards
the resolution of arbitrable disputes outside of court proceedings.
Whereas prior to the enactment of this legislation the courts in Ontario
had a broad discretion whether or not to stay a court action, the focus
has now been reversed: the court *must stay* the court proceeding and
allow the arbitration to go ahead *unless* the matter either falls within
one of the limited exceptions or is not a matter which the parties have
agreed to submit to arbitration.

    … Its clear direction is to compel parties who have agreed to
arbitrate disputes to do exactly that, and to discourage them from
running to the courts after the agreement has been made if they think
there is some particular tactical or strategic advantage in doing so.[111]
[Emphasis in original]

The principle of a stay pending arbitration has been applied to contractual
agreements that contemplate a multi-step dispute resolution process culminat-
ing in binding arbitration.[112]

ii. Statutory Exceptions

There are legislative exceptions to the mandatory stay or referral to arbitration
rule. For example, where the arbitration agreement is "invalid" (according to
the Alberta and Ontario legislation) "null" or "inscribed on the roll" (according
to Québec law), or "void, inoperative or incapable of being performed" (under
B.C. legislation), the court shall not issue a stay.

    The legislation of Alberta and Ontario, like most of its provincial coun-
terparts, also creates exceptions where:

---

[111] *Deluce Holdings Inc. v. Air Canada, supra* note 59 at 148.

[112] *T.J. Whitty Investments Corp. v. TAGR Management Ltd., supra* note 65.

- a party entered into the arbitration agreement under a legal incapacity;

- the subject matter of the dispute is not capable of being arbitrated under provincial law;

- the motion to stay was brought after undue delay; or

- the matter in dispute is a proper one for default or summary judgment.

In Québec, Article 2639 *C.C.Q.* states that disputes over the status and capacity of persons, family matters or other matters of public order may not be submitted to arbitration.

A threshold issue is whether it is sufficient to merely *allege* that an exception applies and that consequently a stay should not be granted, or whether the responding party must adduce evidence or even *prove* (in a summary fashion) that the exception applies. Canadian courts have required more than merely an allegation, for instance that the arbitration agreement is invalid, before giving effect to an exception to the mandatory stay rule. For instance, in *IMG Canada v. Melitta Canada*, Pitt, J., held that there must be a "serious issue" as to invalidity.[113] Thus, merely alleging invalidity is insufficient.

An allegation of invalidity has permitted some creative arguments for those resisting arbitration. For example, in an Ontario case, a plaintiff employee attempted to resist arbitration because his employment contract was governed by Ohio law, which provided for employment "at will." The plaintiff argued that an employment contract "at will" was contrary to the minimum notice provisions of the Ontario *Employment Standards Act*. In addition, the employee argued that the contract was invalid for lack of consideration. The

---

[113] *IMG Canada v. Melitta Canada Ltd.* (2001), 11 C.P.C. (5th) 391 (Ont. Sup. Ct.), at 397. Justice Pitt also uses the phrase "genuine legal issue" at 398. See also *Daigneault Holdings Limited v. Metis Nations of Sask Secretariate Inc.* (2000), 19 C.P.C. (5th) 261 (Sask. Q.B.), at 271.

Court stayed the court proceedings in favour of arbitration in Ohio under Ohio law, recognizing that the employee could still have statutory remedies in Ontario if his rights were not respected in the arbitration.[114]

iii. The Scope of the Arbitration Clause

One of the preconditions to a stay of proceedings or a referral by court to arbitration is that the dispute itself was agreed to be submitted to arbitration; that is, the arbitration clause must cover the dispute in question. The debate on these issues often centres on language employed in, and the scope of, the arbitration clause.

The specific language of the arbitration clause, together with the nature and scope of the agreement as a whole and the commercial relationship created by the agreement, form the basis of a court's analysis of whether a dispute (or some aspects of it) must be referred to arbitration.[115] A clause referring "any dispute in connection with" an agreement to arbitration will be interpreted very broadly.[116] Similarly, an arbitration clause providing for arbitration of "any dispute or controversy" relating to the "interpretation or implementation" of an agreement governing the organization, governance, shareholdings, profit entitlements and employment within a corporation, will cover claims for oppression, wrongful dismissal, inducing breach of contract and punitive damages.[117]

---

[114] *Ross v. Christian & Timbers Inc.* (2002), 18 C.P.C. (5th) 348 (Ont. Sup. Ct.). This case also supports a foreign choice of law and place of arbitration in an employment contract, albeit with an employee with a sophisticated understanding of his legal rights. (The plaintiff was a lawyer.)

[115] *Heyman v. Darwins, Limited*, [1942] A.C. 356 (H.L.); *Huras v. Primerica Financial Services Ltd.*, *supra* note 75 at paras 10-21.

[116] *Mantini v. Smith Lyons LLP* (2003), 64 O.R. (3d) 505 (C.A.). Note that the Court of Appeal viewed the contract as a whole, using other provisions and an important schedule, to support its interpretation of the parties' intentions.

[117] *Woolcock v. Bushert*, *supra* note 59 at paras 5, 21-29.

While arbitration clauses covering disputes arising "out of or relating to" or arising "in connection with" an agreement are considered broader than disputes concerning rights and duties created by the contract, the courts have also determined that arbitration clauses drafted to apply to disputes "under" a contract will be construed narrowly.[118]

Even when "arising from or relating to" language is used, a court must consider whether the subject matter of the dispute properly falls within the scope of the arbitration clause. The answer to this question is not always obvious. Typically, the analysis requires a careful review of the pleadings filed in court and the language used in the arbitration clause.[119]

Canadian courts recognize that public policy favours arbitration and that, where the language of an arbitration clause is capable of bearing two interpretations and one of those interpretations fairly provides for arbitration, the courts should lean towards honouring the arbitration option.[120] In *Canadian*

---

[118] *Mantini v. Smith Lyons LLP*, *supra* note 115 at 512; *Pan Liberty Navigation Co. Ltd. v. World Link (H.K.) Resources Ltd.*, 2005 BCCA 206, at para. 15; *Kaverit Steel & Crane Ltd v. Kone Corp.* (1992), *supra* note 35 at 294; *Overseas Union Insurance Ltd. v. AA Mutual International Insurance Co.*, [1988] 2 Lloyd's L.R. 63 at 67 (U.K. Q.B.); *Denison Mines Ltd. v. Ontario Hydro*, [1981] O.J. No. 807 (Div. Ct.), *per* Steele, J., at para. 15; *Heyman v. Darwins, Limited*, *supra* note 114, at 399.

[119] *Dalimpex Ltd. v. Janicki et al.* (2003), 64 O.R. (3d) 737 (C.A.), *per* Charron, J.A., at 751-752, holding that both the claims and the defences raised must be reviewed.

[120] *Onex Corporation v. Ball Corporation* (1994), 12 B.L.R. (2d) 151, *per* R.A. Blair, J., at 152 (Ont. Gen. Div.), citing *Gulf Canada Resources Ltd. v. Arochem International Ltd.* (1992), 66 B.C.L.R. (2d) 113 (C.A.), at 120-121. See also *Huras v. Primerica Financial Services Ltd.*, *supra* note 75 at para. 18. The British Columbia Court of Appeal has noted with apparent approval that "doubts as to arbitrability should be resolved in favour of coverage" and that "arbitration should be ordered unless it may be said with positive assurance that the arbitration clause is not susceptible of an interpretation that covers the asserted dispute" in *Sarabia v. "Oceanic Mindoro" (The)* (1996), 26 B.C.L.R. (3d) 143 (B.C.C.A.) at para. 28, quoting *S.A. Mineracao da Trindade-Samitri v. Utah International Inc.*, 745 F.2d 190 (1984) at 194 (2d Cir.). The Court of Appeal in *Sarabia* found that there was no reason in principle to treat arbitration clauses differently

National Railway v. Lovat Tunnel Equipment, the Court of Appeal for Ontario stayed a court proceeding pending arbitration where the arbitration clause provided that the "parties may refer any dispute under this Agreement to arbitration, in accordance with" the *Ontario Domestic Act*. Speaking for the Court, Finlayson, J.A., held that the reference to "parties" meant that either party could refer a dispute to binding arbitration. The Court also concluded that the permissive "may" should be read to mean that once a party elected arbitration, the arbitration was mandatory. Failing such an election, the dispute could be resolved in court.[121]

The nature of the dispute in *Kaverit Steel and Crane Ltd. v. Kone Corp.* was carefully analyzed by Kerans, J.A. in referring some aspects of the dispute to arbitration, and permitting others to continue in court. In the context of the *Alberta International Act*, the Alberta Court of Appeal held that the existence of a contract must be germane to the claim or the defence in order for the arbitration to be "arising out of or in connection with" an agreement; either the claim or the defence must rely on the existence of a contract. Thus a conspiracy claim whose unlawfulness depended on a breach of the agreement was subject to arbitration, whereas other conspiracy claims not dependant on the breach of contract could proceed to trial.[122]

More recently, in *Babcock and Wilcock Canada Ltd. v. Agrium Inc.*, a *Domestic Act* case, the same Court concluded that an agreement to arbitrate "any dispute or difference arising between the parties hereto as to the construction

---

than contractual choice of jurisdiction clauses, as both contain an election to submit disputes to a particular forum for resolution (at 152). See also *GreCon Dimter Inc. v. J.R. Normand Inc. et al.*, *supra* note 25, *per* LeBel, J. at para. 22.

[121] *Canadian National Railway Co. v. Lovat Tunnel Equipment Inc.* (1999), 174 D.L.R. (4th) 385 (Ont. C.A.), *per* Finlayson, J.A., at 388. At 390, the Court also endorsed the passage from *Onex Corporation v. Ball Corporation*, *ibid.* at 152.

[122] *Kaverit Steel & Crane Ltd v. Kone Corp.*, *supra* note 35, *per* Kerans, J.A. at 295-297. Citing *Kaverit*, the Court of Appeal for Ontario has endorsed the view that it is relevant to consider whether the existence of a contractual obligation is a necessary element to create the claim or defeat it: *Dalimpex Ltd. v. Janicki et al.*, *supra* note 119 at 751-752.

of this Agreement, the rights, duties or obligations of either party hereunder or any matter arising out of or concerning the performance of the Work by or the compensation to the Contractor ..." will include both contact and tort claims arising from delay and extra work in relation to a construction project. The Alberta Court of Appeal held that the "tort claims are a repetition and recasting of contract claims, and the existence of a contractual obligation is a necessary element to create or defeat the tort claims had to be arbitrated."[123]

While the underlying policy may suggest otherwise, there continue to be cases in which courts have interpreted arbitration clauses cautiously, refusing to stay proceedings where the real subject matter of the dispute was perceived to be outside the scope of the arbitration clause.[124] Thus, creative arguments on the specific circumstances of an agreement or a dispute may still yield results for those resisting arbitration. As examples, a contractual provision referring all disputes about a breach of the agreement by one party, or involving a pure question of law, or limited to the "interpretation" of the agreement, may not be broad enough to include issues such as (respectively) an alleged breach by the other party, or a question of mixed law and fact, or relief from a breach of the agreement.

iv. Extraordinary Circumstances

Some Ontario cases refer to "extraordinary circumstances" where a stay is not granted despite the mandatory language of the relevant arbitration statute. Here, varieties of special circumstances may arise, which are unusual and are typically limited to the special facts of the case. The court may see collateral

---

[123] *Babcock and Wilcock Canada Ltd. v. Agrium Inc.*, *supra* note 1, *per* Fruman, J.A., at 108-109 (para. 15). In *Sarabia v. "Oceanic Mindoro" (The)*, *supra* note 119 an arbitration agreement in a seaman's employment contract was held to cover tort claims arising during employment, requiring the plaintiff to pursue remedies in the Philippines. See also *Boart Sweden AB et al. v. NYA Stromnes AB et al.*, *supra* note 106.

[124] *Brown v. Murphy* (2002), 59 O.R. (3d) 404 at para. 11 (C.A.). See also the matrimonial case of *Range v. Bremner*, 2003 B.C.C.A. 675, at paras 6 and 9-10.

reasons for the application for a stay pending arbitration. Rarely, the court may be uncomfortable with an arbitrator's jurisdiction to award a statutory remedy. The proceedings may challenge the underpinning of the arbitration procedure itself or may be alleged to be part of the very problem for which the plaintiff seeks redress.[125] Or, on some occasions, the complexity of the dispute affects the granting of the stay; this is especially true if the court is convinced that there are multiple issues or multiple agreements in dispute between the parties, some of which are subject to an arbitration clause while others are not.

v. Statutory Exceptions

As discussed above, certain provincial legislation may affect a party's ability to enforce an agreement to arbitrate. Consumer protection legislation and class action legislation may have a direct effect on the right to arbitrate[126] and on the arbitration process (such as the seat or location of the arbitration).[127]

In Québec, the *Act Respecting the Régie du Logement*,[128] arguably gives exclusive jurisdiction to the rental board to decide matters relating, among other things, to the lease of dwellings where the sum claimed or the value of the thing claimed does not exceed the amount of jurisdiction of the Court of Québec.[129] Section 57 of the federal *Trade-marks Act*[130] appears to give

---

[125] *Deluce Holdings Inc. v. Air Canada, supra* note 59 at 150. *Deluce* has been seen in some subsequent decisions as a case "confined to its special circumstances and no applicable to a situation in which resort to the contractual [dispute resolution] process is not in itself unfair:" *T.J. Whitty Investments Corp. v. TAGR Management Ltd., supra* note 65 at 20.

[126] See Ontario's *Consumer Protection Act 2002*, S.O. 2002, c. 30, Sched. A, s. 8 and the discussion on class actions in chapter III above.

[127] See Alberta's *Fair Trading Act*, R.S.A. 2000, c. F-2, s. 16.

[128] R.S.Q., Chapter R-8.1.

[129] Monetary limit of the Court of Québec is less than CAD 70,000.

[130] *Trade-marks Act*, R.S.C. 1985, c-T-13.

exclusive original jurisdiction to the Federal Court to deal with the application of the Registrar or of any person interested, to order that any entry in the register be struck out or amended on the ground that at the date of the application, the entry as it appears on the register does not accurately express or define the existing rights of the person appearing to be the registered owner of the mark.

vi. *Appeals from a Stay Application*

Under domestic arbitration legislation, there is no appeal from an application for a stay pending arbitration. Appeal courts have, however, permitted appeals from an application for a stay where the lower court held that the arbitration clause did not apply to the subject matter of the dispute.[131]

vii. *Interprovincial Issues*

If a court action is commenced in one province but the parties have agreed that arbitration is to occur in another province, the court may also consider the case law on stays of proceedings arising from the court's inherent powers or general statutory power to grant a stay. Although the exact test varies amongst the common law provinces, the courts generally uphold an express choice of jurisdiction.[132]

viii. *Referral to Arbitration in Québec*

The situation in Québec is governed by Article 940.1 *C.C.P.* According to this provision, where a court action is brought regarding a dispute in a matter on which the parties have agreed to arbitration, "the court shall refer them to arbitration on the application of either of them." This provision is not identified as being peremptory under Article 940 *C.C.P.*, which means that, in principle,

---

[131] *Mantini v. Smith Lyons LLP, supra* note 116 at 511.

[132] *Highland Produce Ltd. v. Canadian Egg Marketing Agency* (2004), 358 A.R. 201 (Q.B.).

the parties may exclude or vary its application. The significance of the use of the word "shall" in this provision is that, where all the conditions outlined therein are fulfilled, the court must grant the application to refer the matter to arbitration.[133] The effect of the court's referral of the matter to arbitration is that, from that point on, the court is deprived of any jurisdiction with respect to the dispute.[134]

There are two situations in which the court must not grant the application. First, the application will not be granted where the case has been inscribed on the roll. This rule refers to the fact that a party may renounce its right to arbitration and may do so implicitly. According to this provision, the critical fact for a finding of implicit renunciation is the inscription of the case on the roll. When a party has allowed the proceedings to progress to this point, it is deemed to have waived its right to arbitration.[135] Secondly, the application will not be granted where the court finds the arbitration agreement to be null. It has also been held that the court can refuse to refer the dispute to arbitration when the arbitration clause in question is drafted so restrictively that the arbitrator's jurisdiction would not encompass one or more causes of action.[136]

According to paragraph 2 of Article 940.1, the arbitration proceedings can nonetheless be commenced, pursued, and an award can be made at any time while the case is pending before the court. This indicates that Article 940.1 will be operative is cases where, at the time the action is brought before a court, no arbitration has been commenced but a valid arbitration agreement exists and cases where arbitration proceedings have already been commenced. The decision of the court concerning referral to arbitration is subject to appeal.

---

[133] *Pelletier v. Standard Life*, J.E. 2000-1712 (C.S).

[134] *Wolray Hotels Ltd. v. Québec City Hotel Partner-Ship*, (1992) R.D.J. 349 (C.A.); *J. Walter Compagnie ltée v. J.D. Edwards & Company*, REJB 97-00902 (C.S.).

[135] *Peintures Larvin inc. (Les) v. Mutuelle des fonctionnaires du Québec*, (1988) R.J.Q. 5 (C.A.).

[136] *C.C.I.C. Consultech International v. Silverman*, (1991) R.D.J. 500 (C.A.).

ix. Effect of a Stay Application on the Arbitration

In both the common law provinces and Québec, the commencement of a motion to stay court proceedings (an application for referral to arbitration in Québec), has no effect on potential or existing arbitration proceedings until the court rules on the motion. The *Domestic Acts* in the common law provinces provide that an arbitration can be commenced or continued while the motion for a stay is pending before the court.[137] Similarly, paragraph 2 of Article 940.1 *C.C.Q.* allows for arbitration proceedings to be commenced, pursued or an award to be made "while the case is pending." Given the parallel provisions in the common law provinces, "case" must refer to the application for referral to arbitration.

2. Stays under the UNCITRAL Model Law

Article 8 of the UNCITRAL Model Law, which applies to all arbitrations under the provinces' *International Acts*, also requires a mandatory reference to arbitration where court proceedings are commenced in "a matter which is the subject of an arbitration agreement."[138] Pursuant to Article 8, a Canadian court will stay its proceeding if a party requests a stay not later than when that party submits its first statement on the substance of the dispute (typically a statement of defence in court). It is not necessary that arbitration proceedings be commenced before applying to stay the court action, nor is it always necessary to have complied with the technical prerequisites of the arbitration clause before seeking a stay.[139]

---

[137] See, for instance, s. 7(3) of the *Ontario Domestic Act*.

[138] See UNCITRAL Model Law, Article 8(1); *Dalimpex Ltd. v. Janicki et al.*, *supra* note 119 at 745.

[139] UNCITRAL Model Law, Article 8(2); *Burlington Northern Railroad Company v. Canadian National Railway Company* (1995), 7 B.C.L.R. (3d) 80 (C.A.), rev'd [1997] 1 S.C.R. 5 (adopting the reasons of Cumming, J.A.). The agreement to arbitrate was

An applicant in court must comply with Article 8 by adducing evidence that it is a "party," that the dispute in the court proceeding is a matter which is the subject of an arbitration agreement and that the applicant has applied for the stay before or concurrently with making its first statement on the substance of the dispute.[140] If there is compliance with these initial requirements of Article 8, there are three exceptions to the general rule: the court is not required to refer the dispute to arbitration if the arbitration agreement is "null and void, inoperative or incapable of being performed."

Because an arbitral tribunal has the right to rule on its own jurisdiction under Article 16 of the UNCITRAL Model Law, Canadian courts will usually not make a final determination on any of these issues. The court will also not delay its determination of a stay application, pending a determination of the validity of the arbitration agreement. In principle, Canadian courts defer to the tribunal's competence to determine its own jurisdiction.[141] The scope of the arbitration agreement,[142] whether a party to the legal proceeding is a "party" to the arbitration agreement or a "party" to the legal proceedings,[143] and whether one of the three exceptions applies to the circumstances, are therefore all matters for the tribunal to decide finally.

In the court, if it is "arguable" that the dispute falls within the terms of the arbitration agreement or that a litigant is a party to the arbitration agreement

---

not "inoperative" due to the failure to comply with procedures in the clause containing the agreement.

[140] *Gulf Canada Resources v. Arochem International Ltd.*, *supra* note 120, at 120. It is not sufficient merely to allege compliance without proof.

[141] See for instance, *Netsys Technology Group AB v. Open Text Corp.* (1999), 1 B.L.R. (3d) 307 (Ont. Sup. Ct.), at 314.

[142] Discussed above in the context of stays under the *Domestic Acts*.

[143] See *Gulf Canada Resources v. Arochem International Ltd.*, *supra* note 120 at 122. The UNCITRAL Model Law refers to a "party" while the *British Columbia International Act* refers to a "party to the legal proceedings" making the application for a stay: see *Darby v. Lasko* (2003), 20 B.C.L.R. (4th) 289 (C.A.).

or that none of the exceptions applies, the stay will be granted and those matters will be finally determined by the arbitral tribunal. However, no stay will be issued if the court concludes that it is "clear" that the applicant has not complied with Article 8 because it is clearly not a party to the agreement, or that it has applied for the stay after its first statement on the substance of the dispute, or that is not within the terms of the arbitration agreement, or that one of the exceptions applies. Only if one of those matters is "clear" or it is "plain" to the court that an element of Article 8 has not been complied with, will it reach a final determination of that matter.[144]

3. Partial Stays Pending Arbitration

The court has jurisdiction in the *Domestic Acts* to grant a partial stay of proceedings where the arbitration agreement covers some but not all issues in the dispute and it is reasonable to separate the issues.[145] In these kinds of cases, the facts will determine whether the application for a stay is dismissed outright or whether the court may grant a partial stay of the court proceedings.[146] If a partial stay is granted, the arbitrable matters can be determined by the arbitral tribunal with the other issues or agreements remaining in court.

---

[144] *Gulf Canada Resources v. Arochem International Ltd.*, *ibid.*, *per* Hinkson, J.A., at 120-121 ["clear"] and *per* Southin, J.A., at 124 ["plain"] *supra* note 120; *Dalimpex Ltd. v. Janicki et al.*, *supra* note 119 at 744-746 and 751-752, adopting the reasoning of Justice Hinkson. In *Borowski v. Heinrich Fiedler Perforiertechnik GmbH*, *supra* note 36, at 381, Murray, J., applied the same principle to the *Alberta Domestic Act*.

[145] *Alberta Domestic Act*, s. 7(5), *Saskatchewan Domestic Act*, s. 8(5), *Manitoba Domestic Act*, s. 7(5), *Ontario Domestic Act*, s. 7(5), *Nova Scotia Domestic Act*, s. 9(5).

[146] *Brown v. Murphy*, *supra* note 124 at para. 12.

B. STAYS OF ARBITRATION PROCEEDINGS PENDING COURT

While the circumstances appear to be very rare, courts have granted a stay of arbitration proceedings pending the disposition of a court action. In particular, the Alberta Court of Appeal has ruled that there is jurisdiction in the *Alberta Domestic Act* to grant a stay of an arbitration where the court and arbitral proceedings cannot reasonably be separated.[147]

In that case, the plaintiff commenced proceedings against several defendants including one with which it had an agreement to arbitrate disputes. The plaintiff waited a year after issuing a statement of claim before seeking an order to appoint an arbitrator for the arbitration. The defendant responded with an application to stay the arbitration. The applications were not heard for several more months, by which time extensive examinations for discovery had occurred. The Court of Appeal stayed the arbitration, referring to the policy underlying the arbitration legislation against duplicative proceedings and the potential harm of allowing an arbitration and a court proceeding with overlapping subject matter to continue. In granting the stay, the court relied upon section 6 of the *Alberta Domestic Act*, which permits a court to intervene in an arbitration to "prevent manifestly unfair or unequal treatment of a party to an arbitration agreement." The court concluded that the legislative intent to disallow duplicitous proceedings implies that a party may seek a stay of arbitration pursuant to section 6(c) of the Act rather than a stay of litigation under section 7 when the latter remedy is not appropriate.

An Ontario court has granted a stay of arbitration in a case that dealt with competing motions to stay. The court did not rely on section 6(3) of the *Ontario Domestic Act*, instead granting a stay of arbitration on the basis of "customary principles respecting the stay of arbitration proceedings."[148] The court observed that "courts have long exercised an equitable jurisdiction to

---

[147] *New Era Nutrition v. Balance Bar*, *supra* note 106.

[148] *Deluce Holdings Inc. v. Air Canada*, *supra* note 59.

restrain the continuation of an arbitration proceeding in circumstances where the foundation of the arbitration agreement is under attack."[149] In particular, the stay must not cause injustice and the appellant must show that the continuation of the arbitration would be oppressive, vexatious, or an abuse of process.

While there is no report of a Québec court having issued a stay of arbitration proceedings, it is arguable that the courts are empowered to do so. In granting stays of court proceedings where the circumstances of the case fall outside those itemized in Article 168 *C.C.P.*, Québec courts have grounded their decisions in Articles 2, 20, and 46 *C.C.P.*[150] According to these provisions, rules of procedure are intended to render the substantive law effective and should be interpreted and applied accordingly. Parties can seek and may be granted any procedure which is not inconsistent with the *C.C.P.* or other provisions of law, and Québec courts are endowed with all powers necessary for the exercise of their jurisdiction.

C. "ANTI-SUIT" INJUNCTIONS

Whereas a stay of proceedings is issued by a court in respect of its own "domestic" proceedings, on occasion a defendant will ask the court to restrain the continuation (or more rarely, the commencement) of proceedings commenced by another party in a foreign court or before an arbitral tribunal. This injunction restraining foreign proceedings is commonly known as an "anti-suit" injunction.

The power to issue anti-suit injunctions is part of the inherent jurisdiction of the superior courts in the common law provinces and Québec, and has

---

[149] *Ibid.*

[150] *Kolomier v. Forget*, [1972] R.D.J. 422 (C.A.); *Ville de Montréal v. AXA/Boréal Assurances Inc.*, Québec Court, Montréal, 17 May 1999, No. 500-22-018635-994.

been confirmed by the Supreme Court of Canada.[151] Anti-suit injunctions operate *in personam*, in that they do not purport to enjoin the foreign authority from commencing or continuing the proceedings. Instead, they bar the parties themselves from doing so. The criteria that guide the issuance of this remedy are quite restrictive and Canadian courts are hesitant to issue anti-suit injunctions, due in part to concerns about international comity. In *Amchem Products Inc. v. Workers Compensation Board*, the Supreme Court of Canada concluded that the following criteria must be met:

– a foreign proceeding is already pending;

– the applicant for the injunction has sought a stay or other termination from the foreign court;

– the domestic court is the most appropriate forum;

– the issuance of the injunction would not unfairly deprive the plaintiff in the foreign court of a juridical advantage; and

– had it properly applied the test for *forum non conveniens*, the foreign court would have declined jurisdiction over the matter.[152]

It appears that this power of Canadian courts to issue an anti-suit injunction may be exercised against an arbitration as well as a court proceeding.[153] Indeed, the policy basis for anti-suit injunctions have equal relevance in the arbitration

---

[151] *Amchem Products Inc. v. Workers Compensation Board*, [1993] 1 S.C.R. 897 [*Amchem*]; *Canadian General Insurance Co. v. Domtar Inc.*, J.E. 99-349 (S.C.). English courts, for example, have long held that they have the power to issue anti-suit injunctions. See, for example, *Bushby v. Munday* (1821), 56 E.R. 908 (H.L.); *The Atlantic Star*, [1973] 2 All E.R. 175 (H.L.); *Donohue v. Armco*, [2001] H.L.J. No. 64.

[152] *Amchem, ibid.*

[153] *Lac d'Amiante du Canada Ltée. v. Lac d'Amiante du Canada Ltée.*, J.E. 99-1577 (S.C.), aff'd J.E. 2000-30 (C.A.); *Dent Wizard International Corp. v. Brazeau*, [1998] O.J. No. 5336 (S.C.).

context: such injunctions prevent forum shopping, jurisdictional abuses, and further the best interests of the administration of justice. However, the anti-suit injunction case law in respect of arbitrations is embryonic.[154]

---

[154] For example it is not clear whether Article 5 of the UNCITRAL Model Law has any effect on a superior court's power to entertain anti-suit injunctions in international commercial arbitrations.

VIII. Obtaining a Remedy before the Arbitration Hearing

A. INTERIM MEASURES OR RELIEF FROM THE COURTS

Despite the parties' agreement to resolve their disputes in private by arbitration, there are times when one party must have an urgent question decided by a court. The problem here is a practical one. The issue of whether or not a party could ultimately be successful in convincing an arbitral tribunal to grant an interim measure or relief is not relevant where the party seeking the relief cannot, as a practical matter, obtain that relief with the same speed as it can by proceeding to the court. For instance, interim relief may be needed before the arbitrator(s) is appointed.

The ability of the courts to intervene both prior to and, in certain instances, during arbitration proceedings is not only compatible with the parties' agreement to arbitrate – it is also an advantageous feature of arbitration. Unless parties voluntarily comply with any interim or provisional relief granted by an arbitral tribunal, the award must be entered in the court system to have judicial force. While entering the award is straightforward, it can take time to apply to the court and in some cases, time is critical and even a day's delay is expensive.

1. Common Law Provinces

In Alberta and Ontario, as well as Saskatchewan, Manitoba, New Brunswick and Nova Scotia, the powers of the court with respect to "the detention, preservation and inspection of property, interim injunctions and the appointment of receivers" are the same in arbitrations as in court actions. While for greater certainty, the parties may be tempted to make specific reference to these powers in their arbitration agreement, no such reference is necessary.

In British Columbia, the commercial arbitration legislation is less clear at face value: it provides that it is "not incompatible" with an arbitration agreement for a party to request that the court grant an "interim measure of protection," "before or during arbitral proceedings." But it is clear that the B.C. courts can and do issue interim relief, including *Mareva* injunctions and garnishee orders.[155] The statutes in Prince Edward Island, Newfoundland and Labrador, the Yukon and the Northwest Territories are silent on this issue.

2. Québec

Article 940.4 *C.C.P.* permits a judge or the court to grant provisional measures before or during arbitration proceedings. Book V (Special Proceedings), Title I (Provisional Remedies) sets out the types of special proceedings available in Québec, which include seizure before judgement, judicial sequestration and injunctions. Article 9 of the UNCITRAL Model Law, which serves as an interpretative guide in extra-provincial and international commercial arbitration, adopts the same principle.

---

[155] *Silver Standard Resources Inc. v. Joint Stock Company Geolog et al.* (1998), 59 B.C.L.R. (3d) 196 (B.C.C.A.).

B. INTERIM MEASURES OR RELIEF FROM AN ARBITRAL TRIBUNAL

1. Common Law Provinces

Legislation in Alberta and Ontario, as well as Saskatchewan, Manitoba, New Brunswick and Nova Scotia, explicitly permits arbitrators to "make orders for the detention, preservation or inspection of property and documents that are the subject of the arbitration or as to which a question may arise in the arbitration."[156]

In addition, legislation in Alberta, Saskatchewan, Manitoba, Ontario and Nova Scotia provides that an arbitral tribunal shall decide a matter in dispute in accordance with law, including equity, and may order specific performance, injunctions and other equitable remedies.[157] There appears to be no reason why such equitable remedies may not be granted on an interim basis.

The *British Columbia Domestic Act* contains no express provision concerning interim measures.[158] Nor is there general language in the statute on the tribunal's powers. The BCICAC rules incorporated in the *British Columbia Domestic Act* will apply to domestic arbitrations in that province unless the parties agree otherwise. The BCICAC Domestic Arbitration Rules permit a tribunal, unless the parties agree otherwise, to make an interim order or award on "any matter with respect to which it may make a final award, including

---

[156] *Alberta Domestic Act*, s. 18(1); *Ontario Domestic Act*, s. 18(1); *Saskatchewan Domestic Act*, s. 19(1); *Manitoba Domestic Act*, s. 18(1); *New Brunswick Domestic Act*, s. 18(1): *Nova Scotia Domestic Act*, s. 20(1).

[157] *Alberta Domestic Act*, s. 31; *Saskatchewan Domestic Act*, s. 34; *Manitoba Domestic Act*, s. 31; *Ontario Domestic Act*, s. 31; *Nova Scotia Domestic Act*, s. 34; *New Brunswick Domestic Act*, s. 31.

[158] *British Columbia Domestic Act*, s. 23, expressly permits arbitral tribunals to grant specific performance, and requires that the tribunal adjudicate "by reference to law" unless the parties agree in writing that the matter be decided on "equitable grounds, grounds of conscience or some other basis."

an order for costs, or any order for the protection or preservation of property that is the subject matter of the dispute."[159]

For their part, the BCICAC International Commercial Arbitration Rules of Procedure provide that the arbitral tribunal may order "any interim measure" including security and the preservation of property. Those rules also provide that, except in relation to security for costs, the parties are not precluded from seeking interim relief from a court or other competent authority, "either before the arbitral tribunal has been constituted or, in exceptional circumstances, thereafter."[160] In international arbitrations where the UNCITRAL Model Law applies pursuant to provincial legislation, the arbitrators may, under Article 17 of the UNCITRAL Model Law, grant similar measures of protection.

In either situation, domestic or international, the arbitral tribunal may order a party to provide for security in respect to the request made.

Note that pursuant to section 9 of the *Ontario International Act*, an order of the arbitral tribunal under Article 17 of the UNCITRAL Model Law for an interim measure of protection or the provision of security in connection with it will be treated as an award.

2. Québec

Québec courts have ruled, on the basis of Article 940.4 and other provisions of the *C.C.P.* (for example, Article 751), that only judges in Québec can grant interim relief or provisional measures.[161] However, contrary to these decisions, the record of the Québec legislative debate on this issue indicates that the purpose of Article 940.4 *C.C.P.* "is not to uphold or annul the power

---

[159]   BCICAC Domestic Arbitration Rules, Rule 29(1)(c).

[160]   BCICAC International Commercial Arbitration Rules of Procedure applicable to arbitrations commenced after 1 January 2000 ("BCICAC International Arbitration Rules"), Article 16.

[161]   *Placements Raoul Grenier Inc. v. Coopérative forestière Laterrière*, [2002] J.E. 2002-1183 (C.S.).

of arbitrators to grant a provisional remedy but to confirm that the courts have jurisdiction in this regard, which is necessary, given that the courts are in principle excluded from arbitration. This Article does not preclude arbitrators from granting such remedies when the parties have so determined."[162] The legislative debate is consistent with Article 17 of the UNCITRAL Model Law, which, by virtue of Article 940.6 *C.C.P.*, ought to be taken into consideration in international or extra-provincial arbitration proceedings taking place in Québec pursuant to the *C.C.P.*

A number of circumstances further militate against the conclusion that arbitrators in Québec cannot grant interim relief or provisional measures. First, this runs contrary to the clear legislative pronouncement in Article 944.1 *C.C.P.* that arbitrators "have all the necessary powers for the exercise of their jurisdiction." Secondly, pursuant to Article 940 *C.C.P.*, Article 940.4 is not peremptory, suggesting that parties are free, through the terms of their arbitration agreement, to give an arbitrator the power to grant interim relief or provisional measures. In this regard, it is important to note the comments of the Supreme Court of Canada in *Editions Chouette (1987) Inc. v. Desputeaux*: "[t]he arbitrator's mandate must not be interpreted restrictively by limiting it to what is expressly set out in the arbitration agreement. The mandate also includes everything that is closely connected with the agreement."[163] Finally, there is no support for the argument found in certain Québec cases that arbitrators in Québec do not have the power to grant interim measures or relief because this power is exclusive to the inherent jurisdiction of the Superior Court. Certainly the constitutionality of the arbitrator's power to issue such relief has not been challenged under other provincial domestic acts like section 31 of the *Ontario Domestic Act*. It is more logical and practical to conclude that arbitrators do have this power and may grant interim relief or provisional measures when the relief requested relates to the subject matter of the dispute and is incidental or accessory to the exercise of their jurisdiction.

---

[162] Québec Parliamentary Debate on "projet de loi 91" on 16 September 1986.

[163] *Supra* note 43 at 204.

An application by analogy of principles of administrative law would support this conclusion.[164]

However, until Québec's highest court has the opportunity to rule conclusively on these considerations, parties wishing to enable arbitrators in Québec to grant such measures should stipulate so explicitly in their arbitration agreement.

3. Federal

Articles 9 and 17 of the UNCITRAL Model Law referred to above, apply to *both* domestic and international commercial arbitrations involving Her Majesty in right of Canada, a departmental or crown corporation, a maritime or admiralty issue and other matters governed by the *Federal Act*.[165]

C. INJUNCTIONS MAINTAINING THE *STATUS QUO* OR REQUIRING CONTINUED PERFORMANCE PENDING THE HEARING

What if one party to a long-term agreement simply stops performing its obligations due to a dispute which must be arbitrated, or due to the commencement of an arbitration? Suppose the breaching party is the supplier of energy to operate a facility, provides the critical feedstock for a plant or is a "just-in-time" supplier to a manufacturing facility. If that energy, feedstock or raw material is to be supplied at a fixed or ascertainable price over the long term, the market price (i.e., replacement cost) may be very high. Or the product may not be available at all, if the contract relates to a specialty

---

[164]   *Tomko v. Labour Relations Board (N.S.)*, [1977] S.C.R. 112.

[165]   Note, however, that while it is not possible to obtain injunctions or orders for specific performance against the Crown, the same does not necessarily apply to Crown corporations.

or unique product, or if the buyer is the exclusive local distributor of the manufacturer's products.

In such circumstances, the arbitration clause in the parties' agreement may provide that, if a dispute arises and is referred to arbitration, both parties will continue to perform their contractual obligations pending the outcome of that arbitration. On other occasions, where there is no specific agreement but significant harm will occur if one party can arbitrarily terminate the relationship, the *status quo ante* must be preserved until the arbitral tribunal can determine the parties' rights and obligations.

These cases usually come before Canadian courts in the form of an application for an injunction or sometimes a mandatory order. The courts apply the standard three-part test for an injunction: the applicant must demonstrate that there is a serious issue to be tried; the applicant will suffer irreparable harm if the injunction is not granted; and the balance of convenience must favour granting the injunctive relief.[166] Often the applicant must give the court an undertaking in damages in case it is ultimately not successful on the merits. Where the applicant seeks a mandatory order rather than a prohibitory injunction, the usual test is more onerous. The applicant is normally required to show a stronger case on the merits as the first step in the process.[167]

The outcome of an application for an injunction or mandatory orders is fact-sensitive, but the terms of the arbitration clause will be relevant. It may be much easier to persuade a court to enforce a negative clause providing that the parties shall not take any steps to impair their contractual relations pending arbitration, compared with a clause requiring the parties to maintain the *status quo* (which may be, in effect, an order requiring positive action to be taken). A *status quo* clause may also beg the question, what (or when) is the *status quo*?

---

[166] *RJR-MacDonald Inc. v. Canada (Attorney General)*, [1994] 1 S.C.R 311.

[167] *Ticketnet Corp. v. Air Canada* (1987), 21 C.P.C. (2d) 38 (Ont. H.C.J.); *Axia Supernet Ltd. v. Bell West Inc.* [2003] A.J. No. 283 (Q.B.).

The decided court cases suggest that if maintaining the *status quo* or continued performance of the agreement involves relatively simple obligations such as continuing to supply a product or paying money, then the application has better prospects for success.[168] On the other hand, the courts are more reluctant to force parties to work together on a project.[169]

It is critical to determine what the parties intended with respect to their relationship pending arbitration. Which party was intended to bear the risk of non-performance (or burden of performance) in that period? Some clauses demonstrate that the parties contemplated continued performance, allowing counsel to argue that there is no need to prove irreparable harm because the parties have dispensed with that requirement. Applications for a positive order requiring continued performance have met with occasional success. The courts uniformly apply the legal tests for an injunction or mandatory order, although an order for interim specific performance of the agreement has been granted on at least one occasion.[170]

D. JOINING AND CONSOLIDATING TWO OR MORE ARBITRATIONS

In the context of conventional litigation, the common law provinces' rules of civil procedure provide for joinder of claims of multiple parties where common legal or factual issues arise from the same transaction or series of transactions. Consolidation may alternatively be ordered by a court where two or more proceedings with common issues of fact or law have been commenced. Where

---

[168] See for example, *Cash Converters Canada Inc. v. 1167430 Ontario Inc.* (2001), 48 B.L.R. (3d) 260 (Sup. Ct.); *Dion v. IBC Investments Ltd.* (1999), 2 C.P.R. (4th) 461 (B.C. S.C.); *Toronto Truck Centre Ltd. v. Volvo Trucks Canada Inc.* (1998), 163 D.L.R. (4th) 740 (Ont. Gen. Div.).

[169] See *Axia Supernet Ltd. v. Bell West Inc.*, *supra* note 167.

[170] *Androscoggen Energy LLC v. Producers Marketing Ltd.*, [2003] A.J. 1701 (Q.B.).

disputes are to be resolved through arbitration, joinder and consolidation may provide significant efficiencies but may also be procedurally complex. Some of the complexity is due to the consensual nature of arbitration, because parties who are not a party to the arbitration agreement cannot generally be forced to participate in the arbitration.

The need for joinder or consolidation of claims can arise in both two-party and in multi-party relationships, and in both single-contract and related contract arbitrations. Where a single contract has multiple signatories, multiple disputes may arise between the parties. If the contract provides for arbitration of disputes, it usually makes practical sense to arbitrate each dispute together, as each arises from a common factual and contractual background. Two or more parties may also enter into a series of related contracts which each provide for arbitration. Again, consolidating the arbitration of disputes involving the same type of contractual relationship may make sense, even where the claims arise from different contracts. Finally, where an agreement is a "standard-form" agreement with one common party and many different counterparties, it may be efficient to have one arbitral tribunal decide the issues for all parties.

The advantages of joining or consolidating arbitrations include higher quality adjudication from a common arbitrator who knows and understands the parties' commercial and legal relationship; reduced costs of both arbitrator and legal counsel; reduced management time in instructing counsel and participating in the arbitrations as witnesses; and the elimination of the risk of inconsistent awards or findings of fact.[171]

In most Canadian common law provinces, the courts have jurisdiction to consolidate two or more arbitrations or require that they be heard simultaneously or consecutively, on the formal application of all parties. The court may

---

[171] See, for instance, Rona G. Shamoon & Irene Ten Cate, "Absence of Consent Trumps Arbitral Economy: Consolidation of Arbitrations under U.S. Law" (2001) 12 *Am. Rev. Int'l Arb.* 335 at 359-60.

also order that one arbitration be stayed, pending the disposition of another.[172] The *British Columbia Domestic Act* requires that the disputes be "similar" and that all parties to the arbitration agreements agree on the appointment of an arbitrator and the "steps to be taken to consolidate the disputes into one arbitration."[173]

If the parties consent to all the terms and procedures of a proposed consolidation, there is obviously no need for the court to interfere. The *Domestic Acts* of several provinces acknowledge this expressly, in providing that the availability of court intervention does not prevent the parties from "agreeing to consolidate the arbitrations and doing everything necessary to effect the consolidation."[174]

The *International Acts* in all common law provinces contemplate consolidation of international arbitration, again on the consent of all of the parties to the arbitrations.[175] Under the *British Columbia International Act*, the parties must also have agreed on consolidation in their arbitration agreements.[176] Again, the parties may agree on, and take steps to effect consolidation.[177] In

---

[172] *Alberta Domestic Act*, s. 8(4) to (6); *Saskatchewan Domestic Act*, s. 9(4) to (6); *Manitoba Domestic Act*, s. 8(6); *Ontario Domestic Act*, s. 8(6); *New Brunswick Domestic Act*, s. 8(4) to (6); *Nova Scotia Domestic Act*, s. 10(6). The *Newfoundland and Labrador Domestic Act* is silent.

[173] *British Columbia Domestic Act*, s. 21.

[174] *Alberta Domestic Act*, s. 8(6); *Saskatchewan Domestic Act*, s. 9(6); *Manitoba Domestic Act*, s. 8(4) to (6); *Ontario Domestic Act*, s. 8(4) to (6); *New Brunswick Domestic Act*, s. 8(6); *Nova Scotia Domestic Act*, s. 10 (6).

[175] *Alberta International Act*, s. 8(1); *Saskatchewan International Act*, s. 7(1); *Manitoba International Act*, s. 8(1); *Ontario International Act*, s. 7(1); *New Brunswick International Act*, s. 8(1); *Nova Scotia International Act*, s. 9(1); *Prince Edward Island International Act*, s. 8(1); *Yukon International Act*, s. 6(1); see also *Western Oil Sands Inc. et al. v. Catlin et al.* (2004), 353 A.R. 348 (Q.B.), at 359.

[176] *British Columbia International Act*, s. 27(2).

[177] *British Columbia International Act*, s. 27(3); *Alberta International Act*, s. 8(3); *Saskatchewan International Act*, s. 7(3); *Manitoba International Act*, s. 8(3); *Ontario*

Québec, while there is no specific reference to either consolidation or joinder, Article 944.1 *C.C.P.* states that "arbitrators shall proceed to the arbitration according to the procedure they determine" and that arbitrators also have "all the necessary powers for the exercise of their jurisdiction, including the power to appoint an expert." There is no reason, based on this provision and the consent of the parties, for an arbitrator in Québec not to be able to grant consolidation or joinder.

Consent of the parties is essential to the court's sanction of a consolidation application. In *Liberty Reinsurance Canada v. QBE Insurance and Reinsurance (Europe) Ltd.*, an Ontario court dismissed an application to consolidate arbitration of related disputes arising from four contracts between the same two parties. The court agreed that it made little sense for the parties to conduct separate arbitrations but concluded that "[d]espite the desirability for arbitrations under all four contracts to be conducted under one roof, the court has no jurisdiction to consolidate arbitrations unless all parties agree."[178] Similarly, in *Western Oil Sands Inc. v. Allianz Insurance Co. of Canada*, the Alberta Court of Queen's Bench found that neither the *Alberta Domestic Act* nor the UNCITRAL Model Law authorizes a court to order consolidation without consent.[179]

Given the general reluctance of courts to interfere in the private ordering of dispute resolution by arbitration, it is apparent that where consolidation of related arbitrations is desirable, parties should expressly provide for it in their agreements. In addition to specific terms in an agreement, some international arbitration rules permit the addition of parties by the arbitral tribunal. For instance, the LCIA Rules of Arbitration authorize the tribunal, only on the application of a party, to join additional parties to an arbitration

---

International Act, s. 7(3); *New Brunswick International Act*, s. 8(3); *Nova Scotia International Act*, s. 9(3); *Prince Edward Island International Act*, s. 8(3); *Yukon International Act*, s. 6(3);

[178]   [2002] O.J. No. 3599 (Sup. Ct.).

[179]   *Supra* note 174.

on the consent of the applicant and the party to be added; the consent of other parties is not required.[180]

When it comes to multi-party arbitration, provision ought to be made in the arbitration agreement for the selection of arbitrators. Again, some arbitration rules do assist. The ICC Rules of Arbitration permit the court to appoint all of the arbitrators and designate a chairperson if the parties to a multi-party arbitration are unable to do so.[181]

In drafting a consolidation clause or adopting external arbitration rules, parties should consider the following issues:

– which agreements and parties are covered by the clause;

– how an arbitrator or arbitral tribunal is to be selected where there are multiple claimants and/or multiple respondents who cannot agree between themselves;

– the grounds on which the tribunal may determine that consolidation is appropriate;

– what procedures will be used to determine how the consolidated arbitrations are to be heard; and

– the mechanism for appointment of the members of the tribunal, if a panel of arbitrators is contemplated.

---

[180] LCIA Rules of Arbitration, Article 22.1(h).

[181] ICC Rules of Arbitration, Article 10.2.

IX. Conduct of the Arbitration

A. IN GENERAL

Arbitrations are generally thought to involve more flexibility and a less technical approach to evidence than the strict courtroom procedures. In large part this is true, although the parties may agree otherwise.

Natural justice is assumed to play a significant part in all Canadian arbitrations. Certainly, both sides are entitled to an opportunity to present their case and to hear and respond to the other side. And the parties must be treated equally and fairly. [182] Beyond these fundamental principles (which may be affected by the applicable legislation of the seat of the arbitration), it is the

---

[182] See UNCITRAL Model Law, Article 18; the *Alberta, Manitoba* and *Ontario Domestic Acts*, s. 19; *Saskatchewan* and *New Brunswick Domestic Acts*, s. 20; *Nova Scotia Domestic Act*, s. 21 and Schedule "A", s. 7; in British Columbia, see BCICAC Domestic Arbitration Rules, s. 19; *National Ballet of Canada v. Glasco* (2000), 49 O.R. (3d) 230 (Sup. Ct. J.), at 239-243. This provision is equivalent to Article 18 of the UNCITRAL Model Law, which is a mandatory provision and cannot be altered by the parties' agreement. See the discussion in *Noble China Inc. v. Lei, supra* note 25 at 89-91. The equality and fairness section cannot be varied or excluded by the parties' agreement in Alberta, Saskatchewan, Manitoba, Ontario and New Brunswick.

parties' agreement, the applicable arbitration rules and the arbitral tribunal itself that determine the procedures to be followed in the arbitration.[183]

Much of the procedure used in the pre-hearing stages of an arbitration will depend on what the parties have agreed. Unless the applicable arbitration legislation provides otherwise (typically by express prohibition[184] or by mandatory provision in the UNCITRAL Model Law), the parties are essentially free to determine their own procedures. In institutional arbitrations, the rules of the institution will govern some procedures and the arbitrators (or the parties) will administer the balance. In *ad hoc* arbitrations, there are three typical scenarios:

1. The original agreement between the parties may contain arbitration provisions that expressly provide for specific rights or procedures, such as discovery or appeal rights.

2. The parties may enter into a specific arbitration agreement, or formal Terms of Reference, after the arbitration is commenced in order to establish the procedures governing the arbitration.

3. The parties may incorporate by reference the rules of an external body, such as the UNCITRAL Arbitration Rules, the rules of the AAA or BCICAC International Arbitration Rules. In that case, those rules will govern and be interpreted by the arbitral tribunal.

---

[183] See UNCITRAL Model Law, Article 19; *Alberta, Manitoba* and *Ontario Domestic Acts,* s. 20; *Saskatchewan* and *New Brunswick Domestic Acts,* s. 21; *Nova Scotia Domestic Act,* s. 22 and Schedule "A", s. 7; in British Columbia, see BCICAC Domestic Arbitration Rules, s. 19. See also *Jardine Lloyd Thompson Canada Inc. v. Western Oil Sands Inc., supra* note 43 at paras 18-22. For a comparative perspective on domestic and international arbitrations, see E.D.D. Tavender, Q.C., "Considerations of Fairness in the Context of International Commercial Arbitrations" (1996) 34 *Alta L. Rev.* 509.

[184] *Alberta Domestic Act,* s. 3; *Saskatchewan Domestic Act,* s. 4; *Manitoba Domestic Act,* s. 3; *Ontario Domestic Act,* s. 3; *New Brunswick Domestic Act,* s. 3; *Nova Scotia Domestic Act,* s. 5. In British Columbia, see ss. 35 and 44 of the *Domestic Act.*

In the first two scenarios, the courts and arbitral tribunals will respect the parties' agreement, subject to mandatory statutory provisions and any overriding concerns of public policy.

Questions of law that arise during the arbitration may, on application by the tribunal itself or by a party with the consent of the tribunal or the other parties, be determined by the provincial superior courts. The court's determination may be appealed to the Court of Appeal, with leave of that court.[185]

B. EXCHANGE OF PLEADINGS

In *ad hoc* arbitrations in Canada, it is customary for the parties to exchange some form of statement of the parties' respective positions, either by way of a statement of claim and statement of defence, or less formally by way of an exchange of written statements of position.

Unless expressly waived, the *Domestic Acts* in the common law provinces require statements from both parties to be delivered, which must include the facts supporting their positions, the points at issue and the relief sought.[186] Optionally, documents supporting the claim or defence may be attached to the party's statement. In Québec, such statements along with supporting documents may be ordered by the arbitral tribunal.[187] In many cases, the statements are more detailed than the pleadings Canadian counsel ordinarily exchange in court proceedings.

---

[185] *Alberta Domestic Act*, ss. 8(2) and (3); *Saskatchewan Domestic Act*, ss. 9(2) and (3); *Manitoba Domestic Act*, ss. 8(2) and (3); *Ontario Domestic Act*, ss. 8(2) and (3), which also provide that the arbitral tribunal may determine any question of law that arises during the arbitration; *Nova Scotia Domestic Act*, ss. 10(2) and (3).

[186] *Alberta Domestic Act*, ss. 25(1) to (3); *Ontario Domestic Act*, ss. 25(1) to (3). The British Columbia legislation requires the exchange of statements through its adoption of the BCICAC Domestic Arbitration Rules, Rule 21.

[187] Article 944.2 *C.C.P.*

As in court litigation, the parties' statements define the issues that will be arbitrated, which affects the scope of document production, oral discovery and the evidence adduced a hearing. Pleadings may also influence whether a dispute (claim and counterclaim) falls within the scope of an agreement to arbitrate.

Under Article 23 of the UNCITRAL Model Law, delivery of a statement of claim and statement of defence is required. The claimant must state the facts supporting its claim, the points at issue and the relief sought. The respondent must respond to these points and may raise a counterclaim, if the counterclaim also falls within the scope of the agreement to arbitrate. Again, documents supporting the claim or defence may be attached to the party's statement.

Like the UNCITRAL Model Law, some institutional or quasi-institutional rules, such as the rules of the BCICAC, the ADR Institute of Canada and the LCIA Rules of Arbitration, require the exchange of formal pleadings including a statement of claim and statement of defence.[188]

C. DISCOVERY OF DOCUMENTS AND ORAL EXAMINATIONS FOR DISCOVERY

There is no automatic right to a formal discovery process in an arbitration, at least not comprehensive discovery as most rules of civil procedure contemplate in Canadian court proceedings. Arbitral tribunals have jurisdiction under the *Domestic Acts* to order an examination of a party under oath, and the produc-

---

[188] UNCITRAL Model Law, Article 23; British Columbia International Commercial Arbitration Centre, *Domestic Commercial Arbitration Rules*, r. 21, online: <www.bcicac.com/cfm/index.cfm>; ADR Institute of Canada, Inc., *National Arbitration Rules*, r. 27, online: <http://www.amic.org/rules/national_arb_rules.pdf>; London Court of International Arbitration, *Arbitration Rules*, r. 15, online: <http://www.lcia-arbitration.com/arb/uk.htm#>.

tion of documents.[189] There is no such specific power under the *International Acts*, so the arbitral tribunal must rely on the general power to conduct the arbitration as the tribunal considers appropriate in the UNCITRAL Model Law, Article 19.[190]

In addition, some arbitration rules (such as the UNCITRAL Arbitration Rules, ADR Institute National Arbitration Rules; the BCICAC Domestic and International Rules and the LCIA Rules of Arbitration) provide express jurisdiction for an arbitral tribunal to order production of documents.[191] As a practical matter, most arbitral tribunals will order some form of discovery, particularly in more complex matters, if a party can justify the need for discovery. Some arbitration circumstances may only warrant a narrow exchange of documents to be relied upon by a party and other documents specifically requested by the opposite party.

Discovery rights may be determined by agreement between the parties, or by the arbitrator if he or she has the jurisdiction to make such a determination. Arbitrations may involve anything from little or no pre-hearing discovery, to full oral and documentary discovery, under oath, of representatives of each party and even of other officers and employees with relevant information. Discovery evidence in arbitrations is typically used as it would be in a court action (as admissions or to impeach a witness).

---

[189] *Alberta Domestic Act*, s. 25(6); *Ontario Domestic Act*, s. 25(6). The *British Columbia Domestic Act* provides for production of documents in ss. 5 and 6, and the examination of a party by the arbitrator under s. 6(1). See also *Nova Scotia Domestic Act*, Schedule "A," ss. 8 and 14.

[190] There will be limits to discovery, particularly of non-parties: see the analysis of Wittmann, A.C.J. in *Jardine Lloyd Thompson Canada Inc. v. Western Oil Sands Inc.*, *supra* note 43.

[191] See ADR Institute National Arbitration Rule 29; *British Columbia Domestic Act*, s. 5; BCICAC Domestic Rule 29(1)(d); BCICAC International Arbitration Rules, Article 25(3); LCIA Rules of Arbitration, Article 22.1(e); UNCITRAL Rules of Arbitration, Article 24.3.

D. EXPERT EVIDENCE

Expert evidence is common in arbitration hearings. Experts may be witnesses called by a party or may be appointed by the tribunal itself to report on specific issues, usually after consultation with the parties.[192]

In complex commercial cases, experts are treated in arbitrations as they are in Canadian courts. Formal written reports are prepared and sworn evidence is given on assumed facts that must be proven during the hearing. Provincial arbitration statutes contain no specific rules limiting the number of experts in an arbitration proceeding, although some Canadian evidence statutes do set such a limit.[193]

E. THE HEARING

The time and place of the arbitration hearing and pre-hearing meetings or applications are matters to be decided by the arbitral tribunal, with the parties' input. From time to time as the hearing draws nearer, it is typical in Canadian arbitrations to have several pre-hearing meetings of legal counsel, with or without the parties present.[194] At these meetings, preliminary applications may be made and a schedule of events may be agreed upon, so that the parties perform discovery examinations (if any) and exchange of documents in an

---

[192] See *Alberta Domestic Act*, s. 28; *Saskatchewan Domestic Act*, s. 29; *Manitoba Domestic Act*, s. 28; *Ontario Domestic Act*, s. 28; *Nova Scotia Domestic Act*, s. 30 and Schedule "A", s. 31; UNCITRAL Model Law, Article 26. See also ICC Rules of Arbitration, Article 20.4; UNCITRAL Arbitration Rules, Article 27; ADR Institute of Canada, National Arbitration Rules, Rule 36; BCICAC Domestic Rule 27(4); BCICAC International Arbitration Rules, Article 29; LCIA Rules of Arbitration, Article 21.

[193] For instance, section 12 of the *Ontario Evidence Act*, *infra* note 195 limits the number of witnesses giving opinion evidence to not more than three per side without leave of the judge or other person presiding.

[194] Such meetings are specifically contemplated by the *Nova Scotia Domestic Act*, Schedule "A," s. 4.

organized fashion. There may also be agreement on jurisdictional issues (or the lack thereof), a narrowing of the substantive issues for the hearing and an agreement on the facts that are not contested. Overall, these meetings are useful to streamline the arbitration. They also have the salutary effect of dissuading reluctant parties from commencing unmeritorious motions and arguments, given that the chair of the tribunal (or all its members) hears and decides both preliminary motions and the ultimate merits of the dispute.[195]

At the hearing, in addition to the application of the relevant *Domestic Act*'s procedures, some procedures are governed by the applicable provincial *Evidence Act*.[196] The tribunal determines the admissibility, relevance and weight of evidence[197] and the process to be followed. However, unless the parties have agreed otherwise, the tribunal is not bound by the rules of evidence applicable in court. Arbitrators will often admit evidence based on what is "fair" and "material" to the issues and decide on the weight to be given to the evidence, as part of the ultimate determination in the matter. Arbitral tribunals may also use procedures that are unfamiliar to court proceedings, such as permitting a panel of witnesses to testify together, rather than hearing each witness one by one or allowing evidence in writing by statement or written interrogatory.

Obtaining evidence from a third party is an interesting issue, given that Canadian arbitrations are assumed to be private (or *in camera*) and are a consensual method of resolving disputes – arbitral tribunals have no jurisdiction without contractual or statutory basis. The *Domestic Acts* typically provide

---

[195] The determination of questions of procedure may be delegated to the chair of the arbitral tribunal: *Alberta Domestic Act*, s. 20(2); *Saskatchewan Domestic Act*, s. 21(2); *Manitoba Domestic Act*, s. 20(2); *Ontario Domestic Act*, s. 20(2); *New Brunswick Domestic Act*, s. 20(2); *Nova Scotia Domestic Act*, s. 22(2).

[196] See, for example, *Alberta Evidence Act*, R.S.A. 2000, c. A-18, s. 2; *Ontario Evidence Act*, R.S.O. 1990, c. E-23, s. 2.

[197] UNCITRAL Arbitration Rules, Article 25.6; ADR Institute of Canada National Arbitration Rules, Article 34.

that a party may serve a person with a notice (usually required to be issued by the tribunal), requiring the person to attend and give evidence at a place and time stated in the notice.[198] This permits the issuance of a notice both to testify and to produce documents (a subpoena *duces tecum*). However, the notice cannot require the third party to produce information, property or documents that the party would not be required to produce in court.[199] The *British Columbia Domestic Act*, s. 27(1) and Article 27 of the UNCITRAL Model Law require the participation of the provincial court if the witness is forced to attend. The arbitral tribunal requests assistance from the court and the court will issue a summons to witness (a subpoena) on an application supported by a request by the tribunal. In Québec, witnesses are to be summoned in accordance with Articles 280 to 283 *C.C.P.* In addition, according to Article 944.3 *C.C.P.*, where a person who has been duly summoned, and to whom travelling expenses have been advanced, fails to appear, a party may apply to a judge to compel that person to appear in accordance with the provisions of the *C.C.P.*

On occasion, the law of the place where the award is ultimately enforced may, by implication, affect the procedures used. For example, in some jurisdictions enforcement may be resisted if the tribunal refuses to hear pertinent and material evidence. However, such considerations do not appear to affect the enforcement of awards in Canada and will therefore have little effect on the conduct of most arbitration seated in Canada.

Directions or rulings made during the arbitration are not subject to appeal or other review prior to the rendering of an award.[200]

---

[198] *Alberta Domestic Act*, s. 29; *Saskatchewan Domestic Act*, s. 30; *Manitoba Domestic Act*, s. 29(5); *Ontario Domestic Act*, s. 29; *Nova Scotia Domestic Act*, s. 31.

[199] *Alberta Domestic Act*, s. 30; *Saskatchewan Domestic Act*, s. 31; *Manitoba Domestic Act*, s. 30; *Ontario Domestic Act*, s. 30; *Nova Scotia Domestic Act*, s. 32.

[200] See, for instance, *British Columbia Domestic Act*, s. 32 and *Slocan Forest Products Ltd. v. Skeena Cellulose Inc.* (2001), 92 B.C.L.R. (3d) 230, 203 D.L.R. (4th) 216 (S.C.).

F. APPLICATIONS RELATED TO THE ARBITRATION HEARING

1. Jurisdictional and Similar Objections

As noted above, the arbitral tribunal may rule on preliminary objections, such as a challenge to the tribunal's jurisdiction or with respect to the existence or validity of the arbitration agreement. Most provinces' *Domestic Acts* provide for the express power to do so and the procedures that must be followed to make such an objection.[201]

The timing of a jurisdictional objection is important. Parties are required to act promptly, unless the tribunal considers the delay justified. An objection concerned with the tribunal's "jurisdiction to conduct the arbitration" must be raised "no later than the beginning of the hearing or, if there is no hearing, no later than the first occasion on which the party submits [its] statement" to the tribunal. During the arbitration, if a party believes that the tribunal is exceeding its jurisdiction, it shall raise the objection as soon as the matter that is alleged to be beyond the tribunal's jurisdiction is raised.

The tribunal may rule on an objection when it is raised, or when it renders an award. Where the tribunal rules on the objection as a preliminary question, a party may appeal within 30 days of receiving the ruling. This appeal is done by application to the court. During the appeal, the arbitration may proceed and the tribunal may make an award. There is no further appeal, or application for leave to appeal, from an appeal against the tribunal's ruling on a preliminary question.

---

[201] *Alberta Domestic Act*, s. 17; *Saskatchewan Domestic Act*, s. 18; *Manitoba Domestic Act*, s. 17; *Ontario Domestic Act*, s. 17; *New Brunswick Domestic Act*, s. 17; *Nova Scotia Domestic Act*, s. 19.

2. Removal of an Arbitrator

In rare circumstances, it may be necessary to attempt to remove an arbitrator from the arbitral tribunal. Only after the utmost consideration will an application to challenge or remove an arbitrator be commenced, given the potentially significant adverse effects of a failed application.

As noted above, if circumstances exist that may give rise to a reasonable apprehension of bias or if the arbitrator does not possess the qualifications that the parties have agreed are necessary, the arbitrator may be challenged. An arbitrator may be removed on certain grounds specified in most provinces' *Domestic Acts*, where it is demonstrated that the arbitrator has:

– become unable to perform the functions of an arbitrator;

– committed a corrupt or fraudulent act;

– delayed unduly in conducting the arbitration;

– not treated the parties fairly and equally;

– not given each party an opportunity to present a case and respond to the other party's case.

The latter two grounds have their basis in a separate section of each of the *Domestic Acts*, which the arbitral tribunal is required to follow.[202] This separate section has been characterized by the Ontario Courts as encompassing common law concepts of natural justice, which is stated as an express ground

---

[202] See the "fairness and equality sections" of the *Domestic Acts*: s. 19 of the *Domestic Acts* of Alberta, Manitoba, Ontario and New Brunswick; *Saskatchewan Domestic Act* s. 20; *Nova Scotia Domestic Act*, s. 21. Section 18(1) of the *British Columbia Domestic Act* is substantially the same, given the definition of "arbitral error" in s. 1. Note that in Alberta, Saskatchewan, Manitoba, Ontario and New Brunswick, the parties are not permitted to contract out of or vary these provisions.

in the *British Columbia Domestic Act.*[203] In addition, British Columbia's legislation provides for removal where the arbitrator "exceed[s]" his or her "powers."[204]

In the remaining provinces and territories of Canada, the domestic arbitration legislation provides for removal of an arbitrator on the general ground of "misconduct" or a comparable term.[205] In Québec, Article 942.5 of the *C.C.P.* provides that if an arbitrator is unable to perform his or her duties or fails to perform them in reasonable time, a party may apply to a judge to have the appointment revoked.

The procedure requires a formal application to court for the removal of the arbitrator. On the court application, the arbitrator is entitled to be heard, as are each of the parties. The court will decide the issue and may, if it decides to remove or recuse an arbitrator, give directions on the conduct of the arbitration. If the court removes the arbitrator for a corrupt or fraudulent act or for undue delay, the court may order that the arbitrator receive no payment for services rendered. The court may also order the arbitrator to compensate the parties for all or part of the costs incurred in connection with the arbitration before the arbitrator's removal, although such an order will go directly against the immunity of arbitrators.

The court's decision removing the arbitrator may be appealed to the Court of Appeal for the province, with leave of that Court. The application for leave must be commenced within 30 days of receiving the lower court's removal decision.

---

[203] *National Ballet of Canada v. Glasco, supra* note 181 at 239-243; *Webster v. Wendt* (2001), 3 C.P.C. (5th) 378 (Sup. Ct.), *per* Kitely, J. at 394.

[204] See the definition of "arbitral error" in s. 1 of the *British Columbia Domestic Act.*

[205] *Prince Edward Island Domestic Act*, s. 12; *Newfoundland Domestic Act*, s. 13; *Northwest Territories Domestic Act*, s. 9; *Yukon Domestic Act*, s. 8.

X. The Arbitral Award

A. REQUIREMENTS OF AN ARBITRAL AWARD

The term "award" is not defined in most commercial arbitration statutes in Canada.[206] The *British Columbia Domestic Act*, however, provides that an award is the "decision of an arbitrator on the dispute that was submitted to the arbitrator" and includes an interim award, the reasons for the decision, and any amendments made to the award under that Act.[207] The *British Columbia International Act* is slightly different, defining an award as "any decision of the arbitral tribunal on the substance of the dispute submitted to it" including an interim arbitral award, an interim award made for the preservation of property, and any award of interest or costs.[208]

---

[206] Other than British Columbia, see the *Nova Scotia Domestic Act* which defines "award" in s. 3(1)(c) as an award made by an arbitral tribunal pursuant to the Act. Neither the UNCITRAL Model Law nor the New York Convention define the term, although the latter explains in Article 1 that an arbitral award "shall include not only awards made by arbitrators appointed for each case but also those made by permanent arbitral bodies to which the parties have submitted."

[207] *British Columbia Domestic Act*, s. 1.

[208] *British Columbia International Act*, s. 2(1).

Regardless of the statutory regime under which the arbitration is taking place, an arbitration award must be in writing and must contain an indication of the date and place at which it was made. An award must also be signed by at least a majority of the arbitrators, with an explanation for the omission of the other signature(s) if any, and the reasons on which it is based.

Apart from a formal definition, Canadian arbitration statutes do contain provisions that relate to the arbitration award, such as the requirements of reasons for an award, the granting of interim awards, consent awards and awards arising from settlements, and the amendment or correction of an award.

B. REASONS FOR THE AWARD

1. Common Law Provinces

Except in the case of an award made on consent, most provinces including the *Ontario* and *Alberta Domestic Acts*[209] require that an award state the reasons on which it is based. In addition, as noted above, the *British Columbia Domestic Act* defines "award" to include "the reasons for the decision." Note, however, that the sections requiring reasons for the award are provisions that may be varied or excluded by the parties, either expressly or by implication. Hence, parties who wish to waive their right to obtain reasons for an award may do so in their arbitration agreement. In Québec, arbitrators are bound to keep the advisement secret. Each of them may nevertheless, in the award, state his or her conclusions and the reasons on which they are based.[210]

---

[209] *Alberta Domestic Act*, s. 38(1); *Saskatchewan Domestic Act*, s. 39(1); *Manitoba Domestic Act*, s. 38(1); *Ontario Domestic Act*, s. 38(1); *New Brunswick Domestic Act*, s. 38(1); *Nova Scotia Domestic Act*, s. 42(2).

[210] Article 945 *C.C.P.*

The default position in international arbitration is that reasons for decision are required. However, Article 31 of the UNCITRAL Model Law explicitly permits the parties to agree "that no reasons are to be given." Obviously, the absence of reasons makes it difficult for parties to, where available, set aside, annul or appeal awards.

2. Québec

While the *C.C.P.* does not have an explicit provision that permits parties to waive reasoned awards, parties can waive the requirement for reasons set out in Article 945.2 of the C.C.P. by stipulating to the contrary.

3. Federal

Parties to an arbitration under the *Federal Act* can waive the requirement for reasons for a decision.[211]

C. SETTLEMENT AND CONSENT AWARDS

As in court litigation, parties to an arbitration may, at any point during an arbitration process, decide to bring an end to the proceedings by way of a settlement. Parties to a settlement may wish to have the settlement formally recorded by the arbitral tribunal as an award. The principal advantage of having a settlement recognized as an award of an arbitral tribunal is that it may then be enforced pursuant to the provisions of the New York Convention or the UNCITRAL Model Law. This is particularly apposite in the case of international disputes where enforceability of obligations is more difficult outside the arbitration context.

---

[211] Article 31(2).

1. Common Law Provinces

In Alberta, if the parties settle the matters in dispute during arbitration, the settlement must be recorded in the form of an award.[212] In contrast, the Ontario legislation only requires an award on settlement if a party requests one.[213] While the *Ontario Domestic Act* does not have a specific provision dealing with consent awards on a settlement, section 38 contemplates consent awards and provides that such awards do not necessarily require reasons.

Article 30 of the UNCITRAL Model Law in both the *Ontario International Act* and the *Federal Act* permits parties that settle their dispute(s) during the arbitral proceedings, with the approbation of the arbitral tribunal, to "record the settlement in the form of an arbitral award on agreed terms." According to the UNCITRAL Model Law, such an award has the same status and effect as any other award on the merits of the case.

2. Québec

Article 945.1 *C.C.P.* requires arbitrators to record an agreement reached by the parties during an arbitration in an arbitration award. Pursuant to Article 946 *C.C.P.*, "an arbitration award cannot be put into compulsory execution until it has been homologated." However, since this provision is not mandatory under Article 940 *C.C.P.*, it is possible that parties may accidentally waive its application. If this happens, so long as the dispute between the parties is governed by Québec law, the successful party can still reap the benefits of its settlement (as long as the losing party has assets in Québec) by relying on Article 2631 *C.C.Q.*, which deals with transactions. Because a "transaction" is defined in Article 2631 *C.C.Q.* as "a contract by which the parties prevent a future contestation, put an end to a lawsuit or settle difficulties arising in the execution of a judgment, by way of mutual concessions or reservations," a transaction has, as between the parties and according to Article 2633 *C.C.Q.*,

---

[212] *Alberta Domestic Act*, s. 36; see also *Nova Scotia Domestic Act*, s. 40.

[213] *Ontario Domestic Act*, s. 36; *Manitoba Domestic Act*, s. 36.

the authority of a final judgment (*res judicata*). In Québec, a "transaction" is not subject to compulsory execution until it is homologated.

D. DEFAULT AWARDS

Where a party fails to participate in the arbitration, or some part of it, most of the *Domestic Acts* address the arbitral tribunal's power to continue in the absence of the party.

Where the party commencing the arbitration does not submit a statement within the time set by the arbitral tribunal, the arbitral tribunal has the power to dismiss the claim unless the party provides a "satisfactory explanation."[214] If a responding party fails to submit a statement within the time set by the tribunal, the tribunal may continue the arbitration unless the party offers a satisfactory explanation. However, the tribunal may not treat the failure as an admission of any other party's allegations in the arbitration.[215]

In the case of an unreasonable delay by the party commencing the arbitration, the tribunal may make an award terminating the arbitration, or may give directions for a speedy determination of the arbitration. In both cases, the tribunal has the right to impose conditions on its decision.[216]

In some circumstances a party's default may be more serious: it may fail to appear or may fail to produce documents. In that case, the *Domestic Acts* of most common law provinces permit the arbitral tribunal to continue and to

---

[214] *Alberta Domestic Act*, s. 27(1); *Saskatchewan Domestic Act*, s. 28(1); *Manitoba Domestic Act*, s. 27(1); *Ontario Domestic Act*, s. 27(1); *New Brunswick Domestic Act*, s. 28(1); *Nova Scotia Domestic Act*, s. 30(1).

[215] *Alberta Domestic Act*, s. 27(2); *Saskatchewan Domestic Act*, s. 28(2); *Manitoba Domestic Act* s. 27(2); *Ontario Domestic Act*, s. 27(2); *New Brunswick Domestic Act*, s. 28(2); *Nova Scotia Domestic Act*, s. 30(2).

[216] *Alberta Domestic Act*, s. 27(4); *Saskatchewan Domestic Act*, s. 28(4); *Manitoba Domestic Act* s. 27(4); *Ontario Domestic Act*, s. 27(4); *New Brunswick Domestic Act*, s. 28(4); *Nova Scotia Domestic Act*, s. 30(4).

make an award on the evidence before it – again unless the defaulting party offers a satisfactory explanation.[217]

In cases of default by a responding party in appearing or providing evidence, a key practical concern is to ensure that any award that is delivered by the arbitral tribunal is enforceable. Claimants' counsel should be cautious to ensure that the procedure used by the tribunal, and the evidence on which it is based, will not permit the respondent later to claim any ground to set aside the award or otherwise resist enforcement under the New York Convention or the enforcement sections of the UNCITRAL Model Law or *Domestic Acts*. For instance, as implied by the provision that requires the tribunal not to treat the failure of a respondent as an admission against the party, the claimant must be thorough in adducing evidence and in making legal submissions to support the award. Similarly, members of the tribunal should be vigilant in scrutinizing the evidence and argument before making the award.

E. PARTIAL AND INTERIM AWARDS

When a final award is delivered, it typically conveys with it the termination of the mandate of the arbitral tribunal and therefore renders it *functus officio*. A final award in this sense, then, can be distinguished from a partial or interim award, after the granting of which other matters still remain to be determined by the tribunal.

Although they perform different functions, the terms "interim award" and "partial award" are sometimes used interchangeably. They are, however, conceptually different. An "interim award" typically concerns an issue, such as a legal issue which may affect the outcome of the matter, but does not dispose conclusively of the so-called "merits" of the dispute. In practice,

---

[217] *Alberta Domestic Act*, s. 27(3); *Saskatchewan Domestic Act*, s. 28(3); *Manitoba Domestic Act* s. 27(3); *Ontario Domestic Act*, s. 27(3); *New Brunswick Domestic Act*, s. 28(3); *Nova Scotia Domestic Act*, s. 30(3).

interim awards tend to address the law applicable to the dispute, or jurisdiction. By contrast, if an award finally decides one or more aspects of the "merits" of the substantive dispute between the parties but leaves the disposition of other disputes for a subsequent award, then it is considered a "partial award". As may be apparent, such conceptual distinctions are often very difficult to apply in practice. Both interim and partial awards must also be distinguished from procedural orders and directions, which are often incorrectly termed "interlocutory awards."[218]

Interim awards are contemplated by most common law provinces' *Domestic Acts.*[219] Except in British Columbia,[220] there is no express power to make "partial" awards in the *Domestic Acts*. Instead, in many of the common law provinces, the *Domestic Acts* implicitly grant an arbitral tribunal the power to make partial awards by authorising the tribunal to make more than one final award.[221]

The power to grant partial awards is significant because it allows for the early disposal of a subset of the matters to be determined during the proceedings and can therefore save the parties both time and money. In particular, partial awards can be very useful to separate issues of liability from issues of quantum: the determination of a specific question of liability in favour of

---

[218] As recognized by the authors of J. Kenneth McEwan, Q.C. & Ludmila B. Herbst, *Commercial Arbitration in Canada: A Guide to Domestic and International Arbitrations*, looseleaf (Aurora, Ont.: Canada Law Book, 2004) at 9-14.

[219] *Alberta Domestic Act*, s. 41(1); *Saskatchewan Domestic Act*, s. 42(1); *Manitoba Domestic Act*, s. 41(1); *Ontario Domestic Act*, s. 41; *New Brunswick Domestic Act*, s. 41; *Nova Scotia Domestic Act*, s. 45(1)

[220] See Article 29(1)(b) of the BCICAC *Rules of Procedure*

[221] *Alberta Domestic Act*, s. 41(2); *Saskatchewan Domestic Act*, s. 42(2); *Manitoba Domestic Act*, s. 41(2); *Ontario Domestic Act*, s. 42; *New Brunswick Domestic Act*, s. 42; *Nova Scotia Domestic Act*, s. 45(2).

one party may render discussions of quantum unnecessary or may encourage the parties to reach a settlement on issues of quantum.[222]

Over a decade ago, with respect to international arbitrations, an ICC Working Party expounded a number of recommendations with respect to partial and interim awards in an effort to encourage the harmonisation of arbitrator practice.[223] The Working Party recommended a presumption in favour of a single final award in which all claims and issues are dealt with. However, the will of the parties being the prevailing consideration, an arbitrator must respect a request that partial awards be issued or an agreement that no such awards be issued. Other factors to be considered by the arbitrator are potential time and cost savings for the parties, the efficient conduct of the proceedings, and the need for the decision in question to take the form of an award in order to be subject to challenge. The Working Party recommended that decisions on substantive issues, jurisdiction, and applicable law, but not procedural orders and directions, be made in the form of an award, thereby allowing for scrutiny by the courts. These recommendations, though made in the ICC context, can continue to serve as a guide for Canadian arbitrators in their use of interim and partial awards.

F. EXTENSION OF TIME FOR RENDERING AWARDS

For many, arbitration is an alternative to litigation that is supposed to provide a final and expeditious process to resolve disputes. To ensure that such objectives are achieved, parties from time to time impose short and occasionally unrealistic time limits according to which arbitrators are to render their decisions. For example, parties to a complex multiparty project may decide in their arbitration clause that, in the event of a dispute or difference between

---

[222] Redfern & Hunter (4th edn), *supra* note 51 at 374.

[223] Martin Hunter, "Final Report on Interim and Partial Awards of a Working Party of the ICC's Commission on International Arbitration" (1990) 2 *ICC Bulletin* 26.

them, the matter shall be finally resolved by an arbitrator within 30 days of presentation of the matter to him or her.

While the parties may think that imposing such a short time limit on the arbitrator to make his or her decision will render the process more effective, they may in fact achieve the opposite. The problem with imposing a time limit on an arbitral tribunal is that, if the arbitrator is unable to comply with the specific requirements set out in the agreement, for example, to render a decision within three days, the arbitrator may be *functus officio* – without jurisdiction. Generally, as a matter of law, it will be up to the arbitral tribunal to decide whether or not it is *functus officio* in any given situation. But if the agreement of the parties does not permit arbitrators to extend the time required for them to render a final award, then the only remaining hope for the process may be a competent state court.

1. Common Law Provinces

The *Domestic Acts* of most provinces and the UNCITRAL Model Law permit an arbitral tribunal to rule on its own jurisdiction to conduct an arbitration. In addition to the above, and unlike the *Ontario, British Columbia* and *Alberta International Acts*, most *Domestic Acts* permit the provincial superior court to "extend the time within which the arbitral tribunal is required to make an award, even if the time has expired." Under section 3 of the *Alberta* and *Ontario Domestic Acts*, parties cannot waive the court's ability to extend the time within which the arbitral tribunal is required to make an award.

2. Québec

In Québec, there is no specific provision relating to the extension of time by courts for arbitrators to render their awards. However, there is a specific provision permitting arbitrators who do not render their decision correcting, interpreting or supplementing an award pursuant to Article 945.6 in time, to allow a judge, if asked by a party, to make any order for the protection of the rights of the parties.[224] If such a possibility is there for interpreting, correcting or supplementing awards, it may also be available for the rendering of the award itself.

3. Federal

The *Federal Act* does not contain a provision permitting a court to extend the time within which the tribunal's required to make an award. In the face of Article 5 of the *Federal Act*, it is also questionable whether a party could seek a court's supervisory powers to obtain assistance to do so.

G. CORRECTION AND INTERPRETATION OF AWARDS

The ability of arbitrators to correct any typographical, clerical or calculation errors is important because the principle of *functus officio* requires that arbitrators refrain from re-opening an arbitral proceeding after they have completed their mission by rendering a final award. While arbitration statutes in Canada are unanimous on the ability of arbitrators to correct awards, they are not in agreement concerning an arbitrator's power to interpret his or her own award. Under the *Alberta Domestic Act*, s. 40 and the *British Columbia Domestic Act*, s. 33, a party can request "amplification" or "more detailed reasons." In Ontario, a party may request that the arbitral tribunal "explain any matters" provided the request is made within 30 days of receiving the award.

1. Common Law Provinces

The *Alberta* and *Ontario Domestic Acts* contain provisions with respect to the correction of awards, but do not allow arbitrators to interpret their own awards. Instead, the legislation permits arbitrators to amend their award "so

---

[224]   See Article 945.7 *C.C.P.*

as to correct an injustice caused by an oversight on the part of the arbitral tribunal." Interestingly, the legislation does not require the arbitral tribunal to hear the parties before addressing a correction. This is something to which parties ought to pay close attention, and if necessary, they should provide in their arbitration agreements for a right to be heard before any re-determination is made. When rules of arbitral institutions are adopted, the parties should consider whether those rules allow arbitrators to interpret their awards in order to avoid a conflict between the rules and the applicable arbitration statute.

Article 33 of the UNCITRAL Model Law permits the parties to apply to the arbitral tribunal (or the arbitral tribunal on its motion) to correct clerical, computation or typographical errors and, where they have previously agreed, to request that the arbitral tribunal "give an interpretation of a specific point or part of the award." Unless otherwise agreed by the parties, on the application of a party, the arbitral tribunal may also, within 60 days, make an additional award as to claims presented in the arbitral proceedings but omitted from the award.

2. Québec

Articles 945.5 and 945.6 *C.C.P.* permit arbitrators in Québec, either on their own motion or on the application of a party (within 30 days after rendering the award or receiving it, as the case may be), to correct any error in writing or calculation or any other clerical error in the award. On the application of a party, arbitrators may also render a supplementary award on a part of the application omitted in the award. With the prior agreement of the parties, arbitrators may also interpret a specific part of the award. The interpretation then forms an integral part of the award.

Any decision of the arbitrators correcting, interpreting or supplementing the award must be rendered within 60 days of the application. If the arbitrators do not render their decision before the expiry of the prescribed time, a party may apply to a judge to make any order for the protection of the rights of the parties. The decision of the judge is final, without appeal and, unlike the balance of the provisions relating to correction and interpretation, not subject to waiver by the parties.

3. Federal

Article 33 of the UNCITRAL Model Law, annexed to the *Federal Act* also permits the correction and interpretation of awards as well as the rendering of additional awards where appropriate.

XI. Appealing, Setting Aside and Enforcing Arbitral Awards

A. APPEALING A CANADIAN ARBITRAL AWARD

One of the advantages that is often put forward for arbitration is that it is "final, binding and without appeal." While this statement is true with respect to domestic, extra-provincial or international arbitrations seated in the Province of Québec, international commercial arbitrations subject to the UNCITRAL Model Law, and commercial arbitrations subject to the *Federal Act*, it is not necessarily true in the case of arbitrations governed by most of the other provincial domestic arbitration statutes.

1. Statutory Appeals under the Common Law Provinces' *Domestic Acts*

i. *Overview*

For a domestic arbitration in most common law provinces, a party may, with leave of the court, appeal an award to the court on a question of law.[225] In

---

[225] The statutory provisions are identical for Alberta, Saskatchewan, Manitoba, Ontario and New Brunswick. In Alberta, Manitoba and New Brunswick, the parties may not vary or exclude this right to seek leave to appeal.

addition to the right to seek leave to appeal, in several provinces including Alberta and Ontario, the *Domestic Acts* permit a party the right to appeal an award on a question of law, a question of fact or on a question of mixed fact and law, if the arbitration agreement specifically provides.[226] Under the *British Columbia Domestic Act*, a party may appeal with the consent of the other parties or with leave, on a question of law. However, British Columbia has no provision for an appeal on questions of fact or mixed law and fact based on a prior agreement between the parties.[227] There is no statutory right to appeal or to seek leave to appeal in Nova Scotia or Newfoundland and Labrador, without the agreement of the parties in the arbitration agreement.[228]

Where available, an appeal of an award (or application for leave to appeal) must be commenced within 30 days of the award, except in British Columbia where the period is 60 days.

There is a long history relating to appeals from arbitral awards, dating back to the 19th century and the English arbitration legislation. Until relatively recently, the courts were prepared to intervene to overturn arbitral awards, for any error of law "on the face of the record." This interventionist approach was eventually abolished by legislation. The courts subsequently responded with a much more deferential approach to arbitrators' decisions.[229]

---

[226] *Alberta Domestic Act*, s. 44(1); *Saskatchewan Domestic Act*, s. 45(1); *Manitoba Domestic Act*, s. 44(1); *Ontario Domestic Act*, s. 45(1); *New Brunswick Domestic Act*, ss. 45(2) and (3); *Nova Scotia Domestic Act*, s. 48(2).

[227] *British Columbia Domestic Act*, s. 31.

[228] *Nova Scotia Domestic Act*, s. 48(1); *Newfoundland Domestic Act*, s. 36.

[229] See, generally, J.J. Chapman, "Judicial Scrutiny of Domestic Commercial Arbitral Awards" (1995) 74 *Can. Bar Rev.* 401; *Pioneer Shipping Ltd. et al. v. B.T.P. Tioxide Ltd (The Nema)*, [1980] 3 All E.R. 117 (C.A.), aff'd [1981] 2 All E.R. 1030 (H.L.). Canadian courts will likely not require an error on the face of the record: see *Ellsworth and Kapeller v. Ness Homes Inc.* (1999), 241 A.R. 186 at 196-197.

ii. Seeking Leave to Appeal

Statutory Tests

The statutory test for obtaining leave to appeal on a question of law in several provinces, including Alberta and Ontario, requires an applicant to show that:

– the importance to the parties of the matters at stake in the arbitration justifies an appeal, and

– the determination of the question of law at issue will significantly affect the rights of the parties. [230]

There is considerable case law on the interpretation of these criteria, particularly on whether financial impact of the arbitration award will be sufficiently important to justify an appeal and whether a proposed question will "significantly affect the rights of the parties" if it resolves a purely retrospective dispute. In Ontario, the courts require some "future" or "ongoing" impact of the appeal decision on the rights or relationship between the parties.[231]

In some provinces, a public interest must be demonstrated in order to obtain leave to appeal. Some Alberta case law has imported a public interest test into the statutory test for granting leave to appeal,[232] although the public

---

[230] *Alberta Domestic Act*, s. 44(2); *Saskatchewan Domestic Act*, s. 45(2); *Manitoba Domestic Act*, s. 44(2); *Ontario Domestic Act*, s. 45(2); *New Brunswick Domestic Act*, s. 45(1).

[231] See *Denison Mines v. Ontario Hydro* (2002), 61 O.R. (3d) 291 (Ont. Gen. Div.), *per* Ground, J., at 295.

[232] *Warren v. Alberta Lawyers' Public Protection Association* (1997), 208 A.R. 149 (Q.B.); *Sherwin-Williams Co. v. Walls Alive (Edmonton) Ltd.* (2002), 331 A.R. 317 (Q.B.), aff'd (2003) 17 Alta. L.R. (4th) 35 (C.A.); *Oakford v. Telemark*, [2001] A.J. No. 853 (Q.B.); *Schultz v. Schultz* (2000), 282 A.R. 59 (Q.B.); *Co-operators General Insurance Co. v. Great Pacific Industries Inc.* (1998), 213 A.R. 229 (Q.B.), leave to

interest criterion has not been uniformly adopted by Alberta courts.[233] The Ontario courts deny any requirement to demonstrate a public interest.[234]

The public interest is clearly engaged under the *British Columbia Domestic Act*, which provides that the court may grant leave to appeal if it determines that:

– the importance of the result of the arbitration to the parties justifies the intervention of the court and the determination of the point of law may prevent a miscarriage of justice;

– the point of law is of importance to some class or body of persons of which the applicant is a member; or

– the point of law is of general or public importance.[235]

In Manitoba, the usual test for obtaining leave to appeal does not apply where the arbitration agreement provides for an appeal to the Court of Appeal and the Minister of Justice is "satisfied that the arbitration relates to a matter of major importance to the province."[236]

A Question of Law

Applications for leave to appeal must identify a pure question of law on which to appeal, which is often difficult to separate from a question of mixed

---

appeal dismissed (1998), 219 A.R. 90. This requirement, while not apparent in the wording of the statute, has roots in the reformed English arbitration law.

[233] Alberta cases *contra* include *Rudiger Holdings Ltd. v. Kellyvon Farms Ltd.* (2002), 321 A.R. 182 (Q.B.) and *Alberta Power (2000) Ltd. et al. v. Fording Inc.* (unreported, Alta. Q.B., April 16, 2004, MacLeod, J.).

[234] *Denison Mines v. Ontario Hydro*, *supra* note 231, at 294-295.

[235] *British Columbia Domestic Act*, s. 31(2).

[236] *Manitoba Domestic Act*, s. 44(5).

law and fact.[237] There are numerous recent appellate cases defining what is a question of law as opposed to a question of mixed law and fact, a distinction which (ironically) has always been presumed to be an easy one to make.[238] Interestingly, Alberta also excludes appeals where the parties expressly referred the question of law to the arbitrator for decision.[239]

The British Columbia courts have held, consistent with the requirement to show that determination of the question of law will significantly affect the rights of the parties and with the "miscarriage of justice" aspect of the test, that the proposed question of law must also be shown to be material, in that it must affect the outcome of the arbitration.[240] In this context, it is apparent why judges hearing applications for leave to appeal read and analyze the reasons given by the arbitrator for the award.

Consideration of the Merits of the Proposed Appeal

In addition to the statutory criteria described above, British Columbia cases also contemplate a residual "discretion" when deciding whether to grant leave. This residual discretion arises under the first ground described above, again outside the strict wording of the legislation and regardless of whether the statutory test has been met. This discretion, for many years, required an

---

[237] *Pachanga Energy Inc. v. Mobil Investments*, 15 Alta L.R. (3d) 1 (C.A.), affirming (1993), 8 Alta L.R. (3d) 284 (Q.B.); *AWS Engineers and Planners Corp. v. Deep River (Town)* (2005), 249 D.L.R. (4th) 478 (Ont. Sup. Ct.) at 499-506; *National Ballet of Canada v. Glasco, supra* note 181 at 244-245; *Denison Mines v. Ontario Hydro, supra* note 230, at 293.

[238] *Housen v. Nikolaisen*, [2002] 2 S.C.R. 235; *Canada (Director of Investigation and Research) v. Southam Inc.*, [1997] 1 S.C.R. 748.

[239] See *Alberta Domestic Act*, s. 44(3).

[240] *Student Association of British Columbia Institute of Technology v. British Columbia Institute of Technology* (2000), 192 D.L.R. (4th) 122 (B.C. C.A.), leave to appeal to S.C.C. dismissed [2000] S.C.C.A. No. 564 at 132-33; *Jakobsen v. Wear Vision Capital Inc.*, [2004] B.C.J. No. 502 (C.A.) at para. 8. See also *Kimberley Management Ltd. v. Klammer* (2000), 281 A.R. 158 (C.A.) at 159.

applicant to show that the arbitration award was "obviously wrong" – a very high standard. Recently, the Court of Appeal has decided that, in exercising the discretion to grant leave on a "principled basis" from an arbitral award, the applicant must show that there is "more than an arguable point" on the merits; in other words, that the appeal has "sufficient substance to warrant an appeal."[241]

This latter point is important: as other cases across Canada show, the courts often actively consider the merits of the proposed appeal.[242] This is a clear requirement in British Columbia, not as an aspect of considering whether there is a potential "miscarriage of justice" but as part of the exercise of the general discretion on whether to grant leave to appeal. In Alberta, it has been suggested that there must be an "arguable error" in the decision appealed from.[243] Practically speaking, however, the merits of the proposed appeal may be a critical issue for a judge considering an application for leave to appeal. Elsewhere, as in Ontario, the court's function is said to be limited to excluding vexatious or frivolous appeals.[244]

---

[241] *Student Association of British Columbia Institute of Technology v. British Columbia Institute of Technology, ibid.* overruling in part *Domtar Inc. v. Belkin Inc.* (1989), 62 D.L.R. (4th) 530 (B.C. C.A.). There are other factors in exercising the general discretion, some of which are articulated at 133-134. See also *Jakobsen v. Wear Vision Capital Inc., ibid.* at paras 7 and 11, and *Alberta Power (2000) Ltd. et al. v. Fording Inc., supra* note 233.

[242] In addition to *Student Association of British Columbia Institute of Technology v. British Columbia Institute of Technology, ibid.*, see the Alberta cases cited above and *Pachanga Energy Inc. v. Mobil Investments, supra* note 236 in which the Court of Appeal, while denying leave to appeal because there was no question of law, commented that the arbitrator was not "clearly wrong."

[243] *Kimberley Management Ltd. v. Klammer, supra* note 240, at 159-160.

[244] *Hillmond Investments v. Canadian Imperial Bank of Commerce* (1996), 29 O.R. (3d) 612 (C.A.); *Denison Mines v. Ontario Hydro, supra* note 231, at 295; *Jevco Insurance Co. v. Pilot Insurance Co.*, [2003] O.J. No. 2041 (Sup. Ct.).

iii. Standard of Review on Appeal

The appeal court will apply the usual standards of deference applied by an appellate court reviewing an ordinary trial court in Canada. Thus, on an appeal, an arbitrator's statements of law will be considered on the standard of correctness, whether the appeal is made as of right (by agreement) or following an application for leave to appeal. Findings of fact by an arbitrator are entitled to deference unless there has been a manifest or "palpable and overriding" error. The appeal court's level of deference to questions of mixed fact and law is addressed on a case-by-case basis.[245]

There may be exceptions to these rules, for instance where the parties have agreed on the standard of review in their arbitration agreement, either expressly or by way of privative clause. Alternatively, it may be argued that the arbitrator has specialized expertise to which deference must, in the circumstances, be given. That outcome of that argument will depend on the specific arbitrator and circumstances of each case.[246]

---

[245] *869163 Ontario Ltd. v. Torrey Springs II Associates Ltd. Partnership* (2004), 48 B.L.R. (3d) 184 (Ont. Sup. Ct.); *Alberta v. Nilsson* (2003), 220 D.L.R. (4th) 474 at 494 (C.A.), leave to appeal to S.C.C. dismissed (2003), 19 Alta. L.R. (4th) 1; *Kimberley Management Ltd. v. Klammer*, *supra* note 240 at 160; *AWS Engineers and Planners Corp. v. Deep River (Town)*, *supra* note 237 at 506-508; *National Ballet of Canada v. Glasco*, *supra* note 182 at 245; *Calabrese v. Weeks* (2003), 38 B.L.R. (3rd) 221 (Ont. Sup. Ct.); *Willick v. Willick* (1994), 158 A.R. 52 (Q.B.) at paras 19-32; *Altarose Construction Ltd. v. Kornichuk* (1997), 201 A.R. 258 (Q.B.) at para. 23. See generally, *Housen v. Nikolaisen*, *supra* note 238.

[246] The domestic arbitration appeal cases contemplate the prospect of differing levels of deference based on expertise and other factors (see for instance, the discussion of Lalonde, J., in *AWS Engineers and Planners Corp. v. Deep River (Town)*, *supra* note 237 at 507-508). Some courts have been attracted to the application of the factors used to determine the level of deference afforded to specialized tribunals created by statute set out in *Pushpanathan v. Canada (Minister of Citizenship and Immigration)*, [1998] 1 S.C.R. 982. By contrast, in the cases involving enforcement of international arbitration awards, the foreign tribunal is given considerable deference but the courts have been reluctant to apply the *Pushpanathan* principles: see *The United Mexican*

iv. Agreements to Exclude Appeal Rights

In some provinces, namely Alberta, Manitoba and New Brunswick, the parties may not vary or exclude the statutory right to seek leave to appeal on a question of law.[247] In other provinces (Saskatchewan and Ontario), the statutory right may be overridden in the arbitration agreement.[248] Where an agreement is silent, the statutory right to seek leave will presumably apply.[249]

There is considerable case law on what language will be required to exclude a right to seek leave to appeal.[250] Parties seeking real finality may well want to exclude any appeal rights, particularly if there is a commercial deadline and an appeal would give an unfair advantage to the losing party. Practically, it is obviously preferable to be perfectly clear in an arbitration agreement whether or not appeal rights are contemplated. In many agreements, however, the arbitrator's decision is said to be "final," "binding," "conclusive" or some combination such as "final and binding." The question for courts is whether the chosen language precludes an appeal.

Beyond the ability of the parties under the applicable statute to exclude appeal rights, the question is one of interpretation of the parties' agreement in accordance with their (presumed) intentions. Where the parties language does not expressly exclude appeal rights, the courts have had difficulty. In

---

States v. Karpa (2005), 248 D.L.R. (4th) 454 (Ont. C.A.), *per* Armstrong, J.A., at para 34; *The United Mexican States v. Metalclad Corporation*, *supra* note 30 and the discussion below.

[247] *Alberta, Manitoba* and *New Brunswick Domestic Acts*, s. 3. Uniquely, the *Nova Scotia Domestic Act*, s. 5, precludes the parties from excluding their right to agree to appeal rights as contemplated by s. 48(2).

[248] *Denison Mines Ltd. v. Ontario Hydro* (2002), 58 O.R. (3d) 26 (C.A.); *Bank of Nova Scotia v. Span West Farms Ltd.* (2003), 237 Sask. R. 175 (Q.B.), appeal dismissed (2003), 232 Sask. R. 279 (C.A.).

[249] *Denison Mines Limited v. Ontario Hydro*, *ibid*, at 31-32.

[250] See for instance, *National Ballet of Canada v. Glasco*, *supra* note 182 at 243-244 and the cases cited therein.

Denison Mines v. Ontario Hydro, the parties agreed that all disputes "arising in connection with this agreement shall be finally settled" by arbitration. This agreement was held by a majority of the Court of Appeal for Ontario, over a strong dissenting opinion, not to have excluded Denison's right to seek leave to appeal.[251]

The words "final and binding" in relation to an arbitration decision have often been held to exclude appeal rights.[252] However, the question is always one of the parties' intentions as exhibited in the agreement to arbitrate. In *National Ballet v. Glasco*, the dispute gave rise to several proceedings which the parties agreed to consolidate into an arbitration. The parties' agreement contemplated "binding" arbitration and used the phrases "fully and finally determined" and "fully and finally disposed of" in sending the issues in the different proceedings to arbitration. The court held, however, that the parties' agreement had not impliedly expressed an intention to exclude the right to appeal. As the parties had not used the phrase "final and binding" arbitration and had been represented by experienced legal counsel, an application for leave to appeal could proceed.[253]

v. Appeals from Court Decisions Denying Leave to Appeal

There is no right to appeal or to seek leave to appeal from a decision on whether or not to grant leave to appeal on a question of law under the *Alberta* and *Ontario Domestic Acts*, unless the court refusing leave erroneously declines

---

[251] *Denison Mines v. Ontario Hydro, supra* note 247.

[252] See for instance, *Labourers' International Union of North America, Local 183 v. Carpenters and Allied Workers, Local 27* (1997), 34 O.R. (3d) 472 (C.A.), at 479.

[253] *National Ballet of Canada v. Glasco, supra* note 182 at 243-44 (the agreement itself is at 253-254).

jurisdiction.[254] Such an application will be quashed. There is, however, such a right of appeal in British Columbia.[255]

vi. *Further Appeals to the Court of Appeal*

The unsuccessful party on an appeal from arbitration award may appeal the lower court's decision on the merits to the provincial courts of appeal, with leave of the Court of Appeal.[256]

2. Applications for Annulment in Québec

Under Chapter VIII (Annulment of the Arbitration Award) of Book VII, Title I, Article 947 *C.P.P.*, which applies to awards made in Québec (whether in a domestic, extra-provincial or international context) and which is peremptory where the nature of the proceeding is a judicial one, states that "the *only* possible recourse against an arbitration award is an application for its annulment." Therefore, there is no appeal against an arbitral award in Québec. Article 947.2 *C.P.P.* states that "Articles 946.2 to 946.5, adopted as required, apply to an application for annulment of an award." As is the case with foreign arbitral awards, broad deference and narrowly construed grounds are set out in Article

---

[254] *Sherwin-Williams Co. v. Walls Alive (Edmonton) Ltd., supra* note 232; *Cooperators General Insurance Co. v. Great Pacific Industries Inc., supra* note 232; *Denison Mines Ltd. v. Ontario Hydro* (Ont. C.A., 14 August 2001), *per* Morden J.A. at paras 5-11; *Hillmond Investments Ltd. v. Canadian Imperial Bank of Commerce, supra* note 244.

[255] *Sandbar Construction Ltd. v. Pacific Parkland Properties Inc.* (1994), 87 B.C.L.R. (2d) 145 (C.A.); *Jakobsen v. Wear Vision Capital Inc., supra* note 239 at para. 8.

[256] *Alberta Domestic Act,* s. 48; *Saskatchewan Domestic Act,* s. 49; *Manitoba Domestic Act,* s. 48; *Ontario Domestic Act,* s. 49; *Nova Scotia Domestic Act,* s. 52; *New Brunswick Domestic Act,* s. 49. See the discussion by the Alberta Court of Appeal in *Alberta (Minister of Public Works) v. Nilsson, supra* note 244 and, following amendments to s. 48 of the *Alberta Domestic Act,* in *Sherwin-Williams Co. v. Walls Alive (Edmonton) Ltd., supra* note 232.

946.4 *C.P.P.* for annulment of domestic awards.[257] Theses grounds, which are similar to those that apply to an award "made outside of Québec"[258] are:

– one of the parties was not qualified to enter into the arbitration agreement;

– the arbitration agreement is invalid under the law elected by the parties or, failing any indication in that regard, under the laws of Québec;

– the party against whom the award is invoked was not given proper notice of the appointment of an arbitrator or of the arbitration proceedings or was otherwise unable to present his case;

– the award deals with a dispute not contemplated by or not falling within the terms of the arbitration agreement, or it contains decisions on matters beyond the scope of the agreement; or

– the mode of appointment of arbitrators or the applicable arbitration procedure was not observed.

Annulment is obtained either by a motion to the court seeking such a relief or by opposition to a motion for homologation.[259] The court examining a motion for annulment cannot enquire into the merits of the dispute.

Furthermore, under Article 946.5, if the dispute cannot be settled by arbitration in Québec or if the award is contrary to public order, the court may on its own motion annul the award.

The application for annulment must be made within three months after reception of the arbitration award or any decision correcting any error in writing or calculation or any other clerical error in the award, any decision interpreting (with prior agreement of the parties) a specific part of the award

---

[257] Article 946.2, 946.4, 946.5 *C.C.P.*

[258] Article 948 *C.C.P.*

[259] Article 947.1 *C.C.P.*

or supplementing the award on any part omitted.[260] The Québec Court of Appeal has decided that this delay is a matter of procedure and not prescriptive limitation.[261]

Article 947.3 *C.P.P.* introduces a procedure for the remission of disputes to arbitral tribunals:

> on the application of one party, the court, if it considers it expedient, may suspend the application for annulment for such time as it deems necessary to allow the arbitrators to take whatever measures are necessary to remove the grounds for annulment, even if the time prescribed in article 945.6 has expired.

Article 947.3 recognizes the desirability in Québec for arbitrators to be able to reconsider their awards, allowing arbitrators to take whatever measures are necessary to remove the grounds for annulment.[262] This Article indicates that arbitrators have been accorded powers significantly broader than those set out in Article 945.6 *C.P.P.* to reconsider their own decisions.[263] Article 947.3 *C.P.P.* is closely modelled after Article 34(4) of the UNCITRAL Model Law which states:

> [t]he court, when asked to set aside an award, may, where appropriate and so requested by a party, suspend the setting aside proceedings for a period of time determined by it in order to give the arbitral tribunal an opportunity to resume the arbitral proceedings and or *take such*

---

[260] Article 945.6 *C.C.P.* and Article 947.4 *C.C.P.*

[261] *S.A. Louis Dreyfus & Cie. v. Holding Tusculum B.V.*, [1998] R.J.Q. 1722, 1730 (C.A.).

[262] See Redfern & Hunter (4th edn), *supra* note 51 at 424-425.

[263] See the Report of the UNCITRAL on the work of the eighteenth session held in Vienna from June 3 to 21, 1985 ("UNCITRAL Report"), the Analytical Commentary on the Draft Text of the Model Law ("Analytical Commentary") and the relevant provisions of the *C.P.P.* and the UNCITRAL Model Law.

> *other action as in the arbitral tribunal's opinion will eliminate the*
> *grounds for setting aside.* [Emphasis added]

As the Analytical Commentary suggests, the "grounds for setting aside" of an award in Article 34(4) refers to the grounds enumerated in Article 34(2).[264] The grounds listed in Article 34(2) of the UNCITRAL Model Law served as a guide for the preparation of the grounds set out in Articles 946.4 and 946.5 *C.P.P.* Accordingly, "the grounds for annulment" referred to in Article 947.3 *C.P.P.* are the same as those set out in Articles 946.4 and 946.5 *C.P.P.*

There is little case law or commentary on Article 947.3 *C.P.P.* The record of the debate in the Québec National Assembly on this provision is also silent on its utility and scope. The Québec Superior Court's decision in *Bunyar v. Larouche* appears to be the only case that has examined this provision.[265] That case involved a motion to annul an arbitral award on the basis that natural justice principles had been violated when the arbitral tribunal had visited the premises in dispute between the parties, but in the presence of only one of the parties. In their defence, the petitioners referred, among other things, to Article 947.3 *C.P.P.* Although an application pursuant to Article 947.3 *C.P.P.* had not been made in that case, the petitioners still argued that that provision was indicative of the legislator's intent to restrict the intervention of the Superior Court to the grounds found in Article 946.4 and 946.5 *C.P.P.*

3. Appeals under the *Federal Act*

The comments made above with respect to the application and scope of Article 34 of the UNCITRAL Model Law also apply to arbitrations that are

---

[264] *Commercial Arbitration: Interpretive Documents for the Commercial Arbitration Code* at 163.

[265] *Bunyar v. Larouche*, [2001] R.J.Q. 1942. (S.C.). See also *Learned Entreprises International Canada Inc. v. Lyons*, J.E. 99-1680, AZ-99021798, inscription in appeal, 26 August 1999 (C.A.M. 500-09-008521-999).

covered by the *Federal Act*. Note, however, that while the *Federal Act* applies to arbitral awards rendered in Canada, the *United Nations Foreign Arbitral Awards Convention Act*, which essentially incorporates the provisions of the New York Convention, requires that its provisions govern the setting aside of federal arbitration awards rendered outside of Canada.

4. Private Appeals

It is possible in domestic or international arbitrations to create a private appeal process that preserves the confidentiality of arbitration while providing the parties with a recourse in the event of an erroneous award at first instance. A private arbitration appeal effectively operates as a second stage of arbitration. Such appeals can be to a single appellate arbitrator or to an appellate panel of arbitrators. It is common to appoint former appellate court judges to act as appellate arbitrators.

If a private appeal right is negotiated, it is important that the arbitration agreement specify the time within which the appeal must commence and a clear mechanism for selecting the appeal arbitration panel. Where an institutional arbitration is used, it is also possible to provide that the arbitral institution will select the appeal panel. In addition, the parties should specify the jurisdiction of the appeal panel, including its power to award costs, and agree upon how the members of the appeal panel will be compensated.

B. SETTING ASIDE AN ARBITRAL AWARD (DECLARATION OF INVALIDITY)

Regardless of the possibility of appeal, on a party's application, the court may set aside an award on any of the following grounds under most of the

Domestic Acts of the common law provinces (which are derived from Article IV of the New York Convention):[266]

- a party entered into the arbitration agreement while under a legal incapacity;

- the arbitration agreement is invalid or has ceased to exist;

- the award deals with a dispute that the arbitration agreement does not cover or contains a decision on a matter that is beyond the scope of the agreement;

- the composition of the tribunal was not in accordance with the arbitration agreement or, if the agreement did not deal with that matter, was not in accordance with a province's domestic arbitration legislation;

- the subject matter of the dispute is not capable of being the subject of arbitration under a province's domestic arbitration legislation;

- the applicant was not treated equally and fairly, was not given an opportunity to present a case or to respond to another party's case, or was not given proper notice or the arbitration or of the appointment of an arbitrator;

- the procedures followed in the arbitration did not comply with a province's domestic arbitration legislation;

- an arbitrator has committed a corrupt or fraudulent act or there is a reasonable apprehension of bias;

- the award was obtained by fraud.

---

[266] *Alberta Domestic Act*, s. 45; *Saskatchewan Domestic Act*, s. 46; *Manitoba Domestic Act*, s. 45; *Ontario Domestic Act*, s. 46; *New Brunswick Domestic Act*, s. 46; *Nova Scotia Domestic Act*, s. 49. See also *British Columbia Domestic Act*, s. 30 and the definition of "arbitral error" in s. 1.

As is apparent, the grounds for setting aside a domestic award are concerned with fundamental flaws in the arbitration agreement or the procedures adopted at the arbitration hearing, the fairness of the arbitration and a failure to comply with applicable legislation. Thus, breach of the provisions of the *Domestic Acts* requiring the parties to be treated equally and to have an opportunity to present a case and respond to the other party's case, will be a breach of natural justice and a fundamental flaw usually warranting an order setting aside the award.

The grounds for annulment of an award rendered in Québec are set out in Articles 947.2 and 946.2 to 946.5 *C.C.P.* In examining a motion for annulment, the court cannot enquire into the merits of the dispute. Moreover, according to Article 946.5 *C.C.P.*, the court cannot annul an award of its own motion unless the matter in dispute cannot be settled by arbitrator in Québec or that the award is contrary to public order.

Under the *International Act*s, such as those in Ontario and Alberta, the grounds for setting aside an arbitral award are enumerated in Article 34 of the UNCITRAL Model Law. If the applying party supplies proof, an award may be set aside in the following circumstances:

– a party to the arbitration agreement was under some incapacity; or

– the said agreement is not valid under the law to which the parties have subjected it or, failing any indication thereon, under the law of the province; or

– the party making the application was not given proper notice of the appointment of an arbitrator or of the arbitral proceedings or was otherwise unable to present his case; or

– the award deals with a dispute not contemplated by or not falling within the terms of the submission to arbitration, or contains decisions on matters beyond the scope of the submission to arbitration, provided that, if the decisions on matters submitted to arbitration can be separated from those not so submitted, only that part of the award which contains decisions on matters not submitted to arbitration may be set aside; or

– the composition of the arbitral tribunal or the arbitral procedure was not in accordance with the agreement of the parties, unless such agreement was in conflict with a provision of the UNCITRAL Model Law from which the parties cannot derogate, or, failing such agreement, was not in accordance with the UNCITRAL Model Law; or

– the subject matter of the dispute is not capable of settlement by arbitration under the law of the province; or

– the award is in conflict with the public policy of the province.

These grounds resemble closely those listed under Article 36 for resisting recognition and enforcement of an award.[267] The application to set aside the award must be made within three months of receipt of the award. The grounds for setting aside a foreign award are enumerated in Article IV of the New York Convention. The onus of proof on an application to set aside an award rendered pursuant to the UNCITRAL Model Law is again on the applicant.

In considering an application to set aside an international commercial arbitration award, Canadian appellate courts direct that the international tribunal's decision be given considerable deference.[268] This deference is grounded first in international comity.[269] Consistent with Canadian courts' deference to specialized domestic tribunals, deference is also noticeable

---

[267] Discussed below in section D.

[268] See the discussions concerning deference to awards under UNCITRAL Model Law in *Automatic Systems Inc. v. Bracknell Corp.* (1994), 18 O.R. (3d) 257 at 264 (C.A.); *Noble China Inc. v. Lei, supra* note 25; *Quintette Coal Ltd. v. Nippon Steel Corp., supra* note 25; *Corporacion Transnacional de Inversiones, S.A. de C.V. v. STET International, S.p.A.* (1999), 45 O.R. (3d) 183 at 191-192 (Sup. Ct.), aff'd 49 O.R. (3d) 414 (C.A.), leave to appeal to SCC denied, [2000] S.C.C.A. No. 581.

[269] The Court of Appeal for Ontario has observed that "[n]otions of international comity and the reality of the global marketplace suggest that courts should use their authority to interfere with international commercial arbitration awards sparingly": *The United Mexican States v. Karpa, supra* note 246 at para. 34.

where the tribunal is considered to have special expertise.[270] In the context of a NAFTA arbitral tribunal operating under the ICSID Arbitration (Additional Facility) rules, the Court of Appeal for Ontario held recently that the court's level of deference should be at the "high end of the spectrum."[271]

It is not easy to succeed on an application to set aside an arbitral award. For example, it has been held that on an application to set aside an award on the basis that the award "contains decisions on matters beyond the scope of the submission to arbitration,"[272] the allegation that the tribunal acted outside its jurisdiction must overcome a "powerful presumption" that the tribunal acted within its powers. In determining the scope of the submission to arbitration in *Quintette Coal v. Nippon Steel*, the British Columbia Court of Appeal considered the contents of the request for arbitration, the parties' agreement and the pleadings exchanged between the parties in the arbitration and concluded that the arbitration award was appropriate. The Court of Appeal adopted a standard that aimed "to preserve the autonomy of the forum selected by the parties and to minimize judicial intervention when reviewing international commercial arbitration awards in British Columbia."[273]

It has been held that Article 34 is not a mandatory provision. The right to apply to set aside an arbitral award on the grounds in Article 34 can therefore be waived by the parties in their arbitration agreement.[274]

---

[270] However, the courts seem to be reluctant to import all of the legal principles supporting a deferential approach to domestic specialized tribunals into the international commercial arbitration setting. See *The United Mexican States* v. *Metalclad Corporation*, *supra* note 30 at 375-376 (esp. at para. 54).

[271] *United Mexican States* v. *Karpa*, *supra* note 246 at para 43.

[272] UNCITRAL Model Law, Article 34(2)(iii).

[273] *Quintette Coal Ltd. v. Nippon Steel Corp.*, *supra* note 25 at 227 [first quotation], 212-213 and 217 [second quotation]. See also *GreCon Dimter Inc. v. J.R. Normand Inc. et al.*, *supra* note 25, *per* LeBel, J. at para. 22.

[274] *Noble China Inc. v. Lei*, *supra* note 25 at 86-94. Lax, J. contrasted the *Domestic Act* which expressly (in section 3) addresses the parties right to vary or exclude other sections of the legislation (including the right to "bargain away" the right to set aside

C. ENFORCING A CANADIAN ARBITRAL AWARD

1. Enforcement within a Province

Enforcement of a domestic arbitration award is straightforward in the common law provinces. The party seeking enforcement of an award made in the same province may, in most provinces, commence an application to the court, on notice to the responding parties. The application must be supported by the original award or a certified copy of that award.[275] Generally speaking, the application must also be commenced within two years of either receiving the award or the expiry of appeal periods, whichever is later.[276]

In most common law provinces, where such an application is made, the court "*shall* give a judgment enforcing an award" made in the same province, unless the period for commencing an appeal or an application to set aside the award has not yet elapsed; or there is an appeal pending, or an application made for a declaration of invalidity; or if the award has already been set aside or declared invalid. Where the award was made elsewhere in Canada, the court shall give judgment unless one of the same three conditions exist in the other Canadian jurisdiction, or unless the subject matter of the award is not capable of being the subject of arbitration under provincial law.[277]

---

or appeal an award), with the UNCITRAL Model Law's philosophy, the analysis of mandatory and non-mandatory provisions in the *Analytical Commentary* on the UNCITRAL Model Law, and that fact that the Ontario legislature had not enacted a provision comparable to the *Domestic Act*, s. 3.

[275] *Alberta Domestic Act*, s. 49; *Saskatchewan Domestic Act*, s. 50; *Manitoba Domestic Act*, s. 49; *Ontario Domestic Act*, s. 50; *New Brunswick Domestic Act*, s. 50.

[276] See, for instance, *Alberta Domestic Act*, s. 51(3). The *Ontario Domestic Act*, s. 52(3) provides for a two-year period starting on the receipt of the award.

[277] *Alberta Domestic Act*, ss. 49(3)-(4); *Saskatchewan Domestic Act*, ss. 50(3)-(4); *Manitoba Domestic Act*, ss. 49(3)-(4); *Ontario Domestic Act*, ss. 50(3)-(4); *New Brunswick Domestic Act*, ss. 50(3)-(4).

Even where the unsuccessful party has actually appealed or applied to set aside or to declare invalid the arbitral award, the court may still enforce the award but may do so in conjunction with a stay, with conditions that the court deems just, until the outcome of the other proceeding has been determined. Where a stay is granted in respect of an award made in the province, the court may give directions for the speedy disposition of the proceeding.[278]

The court also has the power to change the remedy awarded by the arbitration if the court would not have jurisdiction in comparable circumstances to grant the award. However, this does not give the responding parties another opportunity to contest the remedy granted; the remedy may only be amended if the different remedy is "requested by the applicant."

In Nova Scotia, the procedure is even simpler: the award is simply filed with the prothonotary of the Nova Scotia Supreme Court.[279] In British Columbia, an award may, with leave of the court, be enforced in the same manner as a judgment or order of the court to the same effect, and judgment may be entered in the terms of the award.[280]

In Québec, an arbitration award becomes executory as a judgment when it is homologated. A party may apply for homologation of an arbitration award by way of a motion to the court under Article 946.1 *C.C.P.* The court receiving such a motion must not enquire into the merits of the dispute. In fact, the court cannot refuse homologation unless the party opposing it proves that one of five circumstances enumerated in Article 946.4 *C.C.P.* subsists: one of the parties was not qualified to enter into the arbitration agreement, the arbitration agreement is invalid under the applicable law, the party against whom the award is invoked was not given proper notice or was otherwise unable to present its case, the award deals with a dispute not covered by the

---

[278] *Alberta Domestic Act*, ss. 49(5)-(6); *Saskatchewan Domestic Act*, ss. 50(5)-(6); *Manitoba Domestic Act*, ss. 49(5)-(6); *Ontario Domestic Act*, ss. 50(5)-(6); *New Brunswick Domestic Act*, ss. 50(5)-(6).

[279] *Nova Scotia Domestic Act*, s. 53.

[280] *British Columbia Domestic Act*, s. 29.

arbitration agreement,[281] or the mode of appointment of arbitrators or other procedure was not observed. Under Article 946.5 *C.C.P.*, the court can refuse homologation of its own motion when it finds that the dispute cannot be settled by arbitration in Québec or that the award is contrary to public order.

A court can postpone its decision on the homologation of an award when one of the parties has made an application to the arbitrators for the correction of the award, the interpretation of part of it, or the rendering of a supplementary award under Article 945.6 *C.C.P.* In such a case, the party applying for homologation can request that the court order the other party to provide security.

2. Enforcement between Canadian Provinces

With respect to inter-provincial enforcement of arbitration awards, there are two options. All of the arbitration acts in the common law provinces provide that a person is entitled to enforce an award made in the province "or elsewhere in Canada" using the procedure described above. In Québec, inter-provincial enforcement of arbitration awards where the seat of the arbitration was in Québec requires, as per Article 940.6 *C.C.P.*, regard to the provision of the UNCITRAL Model Law.

Where an award is made in another province and is sought to be enforced, the *Domestic Acts* of the common law provinces provide that the court "shall give a Judgment enforcing the award made elsewhere in Canada" unless:

- the time for commencing an appeal or an application to set aside the award, in the province where the award was made, has not yet elapsed;

- an appeal is pending in that jurisdiction;

---

[281] In this case, where only part of the award falls outside the scope of the arbitration agreement, the court can homologate the arbitration award save that part, if it can be dissociated from the rest.

- the award has been set aside; or
- the subject matter of the award is not capable of being the subject of arbitration under provincial law in the enforcing province.

The other alternative for enforcement is under the *Reciprocal Enforcement of Judgments Act* ("REJA") applicable in each province. All Canadian provinces have legislation based on a uniform act that allows a judgment in another province to be registered quickly and simply in the enforcing province. In that legislation, a "judgment" is defined to include "an award in an arbitration proceeding if the award, under the law in force in the jurisdiction where it was made, has become enforceable in the same manner as a judgment given by a court in that jurisdiction …" Thus, if an arbitration award has been registered in one province, it may be registered under the REJA legislation of any other province.

The procedure requires that the enforcing party makes an application to the superior court of the province to register the judgment. This application is done on an *ex parte* basis, assuming that certain procedural requirements were followed when the original arbitration was commenced. The application must also be supported by a certificate from the other province's court certifying that all necessary procedures were followed in the original arbitration.

Although it is often assumed that REJA legislation only applies between provinces within Canada, some provinces have in fact extended the legislation. Alberta's REJA applies not only to Canadian provinces and territories but also to Australia and to the American states neighbouring Alberta, Washington, Idaho and Montana.[282] Prince Edward Island includes the State of Washington as a reciprocating state for purposes of its REJA, Newfoundland includes all

---

[282] See *Reciprocal Enforcement of Judgments Act*, R.S.A. 1980, c. R-6 and the *Reciprocating Jurisdictions Regulation*, A.R. 344/95, s. 1.

of Australia's states and territories, and Yukon includes the Australian states of Western Australia and Queensland.[283]

For Québec, arbitration awards rendered in other provinces are, for the purposes of recognition and enforcement, treated in the same manner as awards rendered in foreign countries. The law governing such recognition and enforcement is discussed in part D, "Enforcing a Foreign Arbitral Award in Canada," below.

3. International Enforcement of a Canadian Arbitral Award

As noted above, arbitral awards granted in Canada may be enforced elsewhere in the world according to the laws of the country where enforcement is desired and under treaties entered into between the foreign state and Canada or a province. If the foreign state is a party to the New York Convention or a jurisdiction which has enacted legislation based on the UNCITRAL Model Law, enforcement of a Canadian arbitral award abroad will usually be simpler than enforcing a Canadian court judgment.

D. ENFORCING A FOREIGN ARBITRAL AWARD IN CANADA

1. Common Law Provinces and the *Federal Act*

A mechanism is in place to recognize and enforce arbitral awards obtained outside of Canada in all common law provinces, in Québec, and under the *Federal Act* through their adoption (or reference in Québec) of the UNCITRAL Model Law or the New York Convention. Articles 35 and 36 of the Schedule

---

[283] Several provinces and territories have also enacted legislation implementing the Canada-United Kingdom Convention on the Reciprocal Recognition and Enforcement of Judgments: see for example *Reciprocal Enforcement of Judgments (U.K.) Act* (Ontario), R.S.O. 1990, c. R.6 and *International Conventions Implementation Act* (Alberta), R.S.A. 2000, c. I-6.

to the *Alberta* and *Ontario International Act*s, for instance, govern the recognition and enforcement of foreign arbitral awards in those provinces. Comparable provisions exist in the other common law provinces and under the *Federal Act*.[284]

---

[284] The following provinces adopted the New York Convention as part of provincial law:

B.C.: *Foreign Arbitral Awards Act*, R.S.B.C. 1996, c. 154, s. 2; Alberta: *Alberta International Act*; s. 2(1); Saskatchewan: *Enforcement of Foreign Arbitral Awards Act*, S.S. 1996, c. E-9.12, s. 4; Manitoba*: Manitoba International Act*, s. 2(1); Ontario: Originally, Ontario adopted the New York Convention but in 1990 the *Foreign Arbitral Awards Act*, 1986, S.O. 1986 c. 25 was repealed because of a perceived overlap with the *Ontario International Act*. However, some commentators have suggested that an argument could be made that it is still implicitly part of the *Ontario International Act*; New Brunswick: *New Brunswick International Act*, s. 2(1); Nova Scotia: *Nova Scotia International Act*, s. 3(1); P.E.I.: *Prince Edward Island International Act*, s. 2(1); Newfoundland and Labrador: *Newfoundland International Act*, s. 3(1); Yukon: *Foreign Arbitral Awards Act*, R.S.Y. 2002, c. 93, s. 2; Northwest Territories and Nunavut: *Northwest Territories International Act*, s. 4(1).

The *Federal Act*, *supra* note 32 adopts the UNCITRAL Model Law in s. 5(1). The following provinces adopted the UNCITRAL Model Law:

Alberta: *Alberta International Act*, s. 4; Saskatchewan: *Saskatchewan International Arbitration Act*, s. 3; Manitoba: *Manitoba International Act*, s. 4(1); Ontario: *Ontario International Act*, s. 2(1); Québec: The Québec *Code of Civil Procedure*, Article 940.6, does not expressly adopt the UNCITRAL Model Law, rather, it states that the UNCITRAL Model Law should be considered for the interpretation of matters of extra-provincial or international trade; New Brunswick: *New Brunswick International Act*, s. 4(1); Nova Scotia: *Nova Scotia International Act*, s. 5(1); P.E.I.: *Prince Edward Island International Act*, s. 4(1); Newfoundland & Labrador: *Newfoundland International Act*, s. 5(1); Yukon: *Yukon International Act*, s. 2(1); Northwest Territories and Nunavut: *Northwest Territories International Act*, s. 7(1). The *British Columbia International Act* does not expressly adopt the UNCITRAL Model law but refers to it in the Preamble as "a consensus of views" on judicial intervention in international commercial arbitration. The *British Columbia International Act* is essentially a reworked version of the UNCITRAL Model Law.

Where a party applies for recognition and enforcement of an award and supplies the court with the award and the arbitration agreement, recognition and enforcement of a foreign arbitration award is mandatory under Article 35 of the UNCITRAL Model Law.[285]

According to Article 36, enforcement of a foreign arbitral award may only[286] be declined where:

(i) a party to the arbitration agreement referred to in Article 7 was under some incapacity; or the said agreement is not valid under the law to which the parties have subjected it or, failing any indication thereon, under the law of the country where the award was made; or

(ii) the party against whom the award is invoked was not given proper notice of the appointment of an arbitrator or of the arbitral proceedings or was otherwise unable to present his case; or

(iii) the award deals with a dispute not contemplated by or not falling within the terms of the submission to arbitration, or it contains decisions on matters beyond the scope of the submission to arbitration, provided that, if the decisions on matters submitted to arbitration can be separated from those not so submitted, only that part of the award which contains decisions on matters submitted to arbitration may be recognized and enforced; or

(iv) the composition of the arbitral tribunal or the arbitral procedure was not in accordance with the agreement of the parties or, failing such

---

[285] *Corporacion Transnacional de Inversiones, S.A. de C.V. v. STET International, S.p.A.*, *supra* note 267; *Schreter v. Gasmac Inc.* (1992), 7 O.R. (3d) 608 (Ont. Gen. Div). For consideration on what constitutes an arbitration agreement for these purposes, see *Proctor v. Schellenberg* (2002), 30 B.L.R. (3d) 1 (Man. C.A.), *per* Hamilton, J.A., in which the court adopted a flexible approach consistent with the overall purposes of the New York Convention.

[286] *Dunhill Personnel System Inc. v. Dunhill Temps Edmonton Ltd.* (1993), *supra* note 35, *per* Marshall, J., at 243.

agreement, was not in accordance with the law of the country where the arbitration took place; or

(v) the award has not yet become binding on the parties or has been set aside or suspended by a court of the country in which, or under the law of which, that award was made.

The onus is not on the party seeking to enforce the award to prove that it is enforceable. Rather the party resisting enforcement must demonstrate that the award should not be enforced based on one or more of the grounds listed above.[287]

Further, under Article 36 a court may also refuse to enforce a foreign arbitral award if it finds that:

– the subject matter of the dispute is not capable of settlement by arbitration under the law of the province; or

– the recognition or enforcement of the award would be contrary to the public policy of the province.

The New York Convention contains the same grounds for the refusal to enforce a foreign arbitral award (in fact, the grounds for refusing to enforce a foreign arbitral award in the UNCITRAL Model Law are derived from the New York Convention). Thus, regardless of whether a common law province has adopted the UNCITRAL Model Law or New York Convention to govern the enforcement of foreign arbitral awards, the grounds for refusing the enforcement of such an award are the same across the common law provinces and at the federal level.

---

[287] *Karaha v. Perusahaan* (2004), 3 C.P.C. (6th) 278 (Alta. Master), at 283. See *Javor v. Francoeur* (2003), 13 B.C.L.R. (4th) 195 (S.C.), aff'd (2004), 25 B.C.L.R. (4th) 114 (C.A.), holding that a foreign arbitral award cannot be enforced against a person who was not a party to the arbitration agreement.

Courts in the common law provinces are generally reticent to refuse enforcement of a foreign arbitral award. Appellate courts have expressed concerns for international comity, respect for the capacities of foreign and transnational tribunals, respect for the integrity of the arbitration process and the need for predictability in the resolution of international commercial disputes.[288] This deferential approach also stems from a realization by Canadian courts that the dispute resolution mechanism specifically chosen by the parties ought to be respected.[289]

As noted above, Canadian courts will not decline to enforce foreign arbitral awards based on a claim that the arbitral tribunal that rendered the award made a legal or factual error on the merits of the claim.[290]

The grounds for resisting enforcement of a foreign arbitral award that are enumerated in the UNCITRAL Model Law or the New York Convention have been treated narrowly by the courts, although both procedural and substantive notions of justice will be considered.[291]

---

[288] See *Quintette Coal Ltd. v. Nippon Steel Corp.*, *supra* note 25 at 215; *United Mexican States v. Karpa*, *supra* note 246 at 454. The British Columbia Court of Appeal in *Quintette* (which concerned an application to set aside an award under UNCITRAL Model Law, Article 34(2)) relied on reasoning of Blackmun, J., of the United States Supreme Court in *Mitsubishi Motors Corporation v Soler Chrysler-Plymouth Inc.*, 50 US 614 (1985), at 623: "... we conclude that concerns of international comity, respect for the capacities of foreign and transnational tribunals, and sensitivity to the need of the international commercial system for predictability in the resolution of disputes require that we enforce the parties' agreement, even assuming that a contrary result would be forthcoming in a domestic context." Similar remarks were made by the Supreme Court of Canada in *GreCon Dimter Inc. v. J.R. Normand Inc. et al.*, *supra* note 25, *per* LeBel, J. at para. 22.

[289] See the cases discussing deference cited *supra* note 268.

[290] *Schreter v. Gasmac Inc.*, *supra* note 285 at 623; *Corporacion Transnacional de Inversiones, S.A. de C.V. v. STET International, S.p.A*, *supra* note 268 at 192 and 203.

[291] *Corporacion Transnacional de Inversiones, S.A. de C.V. v. STET International, S.p.A*, *ibid.* at 192 and 194.

The provision that allows a court to refuse enforcement of an award based on public policy grounds has been interpreted by the Court of Appeal for Ontario as applying only in circumstances where the recognition or enforcement of the award would "offend the principles of justice and fairness in a fundamental way."[292] In that case, *Corporacion Transnacional de Inversiones, S.A. de C.V. v. STET International, S.p.A*, the Court endorsed the following statement:

> The concept of imposing our public policy on foreign awards is to guard against enforcement of an award which offends our local principles of justice and fairness in a fundamental way, and in a way which the parties could attribute to the fact that the award was made in another jurisdiction where the procedural or substantive rules diverge markedly from our own, or where there was ignorance or corruption on the part of the tribunal which could not be seen to be tolerated or condoned by our courts.[293]

In the result, the Court of Appeal upheld an order to enforce a foreign award where the respondent withdrew from the arbitration. Given the applicable terms of the UNCITRAL Model Law and the ICC Rules of Arbitration, the Court concluded that "[i]t hardly offends our notions of fundamental justice if a party that had the opportunity to present its case and meet the opposing case forfeits that opportunity by withdrawing from the arbitration." The Court of Appeal urged restraint in using public policy grounds to refuse to enforce foreign arbitral awards.[294]

---

[292] *Ibid.*, at 414-415 [quotation at 415*a*] quoting *Schreter v. Gasmac Inc., supra* note 285, *per* Feldman, J. (now J.A.), at 623.

[293] *Ibid.* at 414, quoting *Schreter v. Gasmac Inc., supra* note 284 at 623. The Court of Appeal applied the same passage in *United Mexican States v. Karpa, supra* note 246 at 460.

[294] *Ibid.* at 415-16.

Responding to the submission that a foreign arbitration award that was under appeal should not be enforced because it was not yet "binding" on the parties,[295] an Ontario court has held that an award need not be "final" at the place of arbitration, although it must be binding on the parties. The court allowed the applicant to enter judgment arising from the Polish arbitration award, but ordered that it "remain provisional" pending the appeal of another application concerning the same arbitration in the Ontario courts.[296]

Procedurally, the party seeking enforcement of a foreign arbitral award may commence proceedings by way of an application supported by an affidavit, for instance under Rules 14 and 38 of Ontario's *Rules of Civil Procedure* or by way of Originating Notice under Rule 410 of the Alberta *Rules of Court*.[297]

Where a party has commenced an application in the courts of the place where the arbitration occurred to set aside or suspend an award rendered in that foreign jurisdiction, the courts in the common law provinces have jurisdiction to adjourn the Canadian application for enforcement and order the provision of appropriate security.[298] Whether conditions can be placed on enforcement of a foreign award, such as the payment of the amount of the award by the unsuccessful party and posting of security by the victor, has not been settled by the courts.[299]

A British Columbia court has held that a party may waive its right to resist recognition and enforcement of an award on the grounds in s. 36 of the

---

[295] UNCITRAL Model Law, Article 36(1)(a)(v).

[296] *Argos Trading Spolka z.o.o. v. Dalimpex Ltd.* (2001), 14 C.P.C. (5th) 134 (Ont. Sup. Ct.), at 138. See *Dalimpex Ltd. v. Janicki et al.*, *supra* note 119 at 745.

[297] *Schreter v. Gasmac Inc.*, *supra* note 285 at 615-616.

[298] UNCITRAL Model Law, Article 36(2).

[299] See *Powerex Corp. v. Alcan Inc.*, [2004] B.C.S.C. 876, leave to appeal granted [2004] B.C.J. No. 2029 (C.A.) (according to newspaper accounts, the matter subsequently settled).

British Columbia International Act (the section equivalent to Article 36 of the UNCITRAL Model Law).[300]

2. Québec

The enforcement of a foreign arbitral award in Québec is governed by Book VII, Title II of the *C.C.P.* Although Québec has not specifically adopted the New York Convention, the *C.C.P.* holds that the interpretation of its provisions dealing with the recognition and enforcement of foreign arbitral awards should take into account the New York Convention. It is important to note that, pursuant to Québec law, any arbitral award made outside of Québec is considered a foreign award, including awards made in another Canadian province.

Article 950 *C.C.P.* enumerates the grounds upon which a foreign arbitral award may be resisted in Québec:

> **950.** A party against whom an arbitration award is invoked may object to its recognition and execution by establishing that
>
> (1) one of the parties was not qualified to enter into the arbitration agreement;
>
> (2) the arbitration agreement is invalid under the law elected by the parties or, failing any indication in that regard, under the laws of the place where the arbitration award was made;
>
> (3) the party against whom the award is invoked was not given proper notice of the appointment of an arbitrator or of the arbitration proceedings or was otherwise unable to present his case;
>
> (4) the award deals with a dispute not contemplated by or not falling within the terms of the arbitration agreement, or

---

[300] *Food Services of America Inc. v. Pan Pacific Specialities Ltd.* (1997), 32 B.C.L.R. (3d) 355 (S.C.).

it contains decisions on matters beyond the scope of the agreement;

(5)   the manner in which the arbitrators were appointed or the arbitration procedure did not conform with the agreement of the parties or, if there was not agreement, with the laws of the place where the arbitration took place; or

(6)   the arbitration award has not yet become binding on the parties or has been set aside or suspended by a competent authority of the place or pursuant to the laws of the place in which the arbitration award was made.

In the case of subparagraph 4 of the first paragraph, if the irregular provision of the arbitration award described in that paragraph can be dissociated from the rest, the rest may be recognized and declared executory.

According to Article 949 *C.C.P.*, an arbitration award shall be enforced if the matter in dispute is one that may be settled by arbitration in Québec *and* if its recognition and execution are not contrary to public order. As indicated above, the grounds for refusing to enforce a foreign arbitral award in Québec are similar to those found in the common law provinces, especially when one considers that the provisions of the *C.C.P.* in this regard are to be interpreted in light of the New York Convention. Although there is less case law on the interpretation of the provisions for the enforcement of a foreign arbitral award under Québec law than in some of the common law provinces, one could expect the Québec courts to take a similar narrow interpretation of the grounds for refusal as courts have in the common law provinces.

The application for recognition and enforcement of foreign arbitral awards in Québec is done by way of motion for homologation. The court examining an application for recognition and execution of the arbitration award is not permitted to enquire into the merits of the dispute.

Article 949.1 *C.C.P.* requires that the application for recognition and execution of an award rendered outside Québec be made by way of a motion for homologation to the court, which would have had competence in Québec to decide the matter in dispute submitted to the arbitrators.[301] This rather unique local requirement cannot be found in either the UNCITRAL Model Law or the New York Convention. The interesting, but as yet unanswered, question that flows from examining this provision is: does Article 949.1 *C.C.P.*, either intentionally or inadvertently, trigger the application of Title III, "International Jurisdiction of Quebec Authorities" and in particular Article 3148 *C.C.Q.* found under Book Ten (Private International Law) of the *C.C.Q.*?[302]

Article 3148 *C.C.Q.* states:

> **3148.** In personal actions of a patrimonial nature, a Quebec authority has jurisdiction where
>
> (1) the defendant has his domicile or his residence in Quebec;
>
> (2) the defendant is a legal person, is not domiciled in Quebec but has an establishment in Quebec, *and the dispute relates to its activities in Quebec*;

---

[301] Article 949.1 *C.C.P.* The Quebec Superior Court has held that the C.C.P. does not permit the annulment of foreign arbitral awards: *Domotique Secant Inc. v. Smart Systems Technologies Inc. et al*, J.E. 2005-2114 (C.S.) (appeal pending).

[302] See also Jean Gabriel Castel & Janet Walker, *Canadian Conflict of Laws*, 6th edn (Toronto: Butterworths, 2005) at 15-59 where a similar question is raised by the authors. There are also two Québec decisions (*C.I.C. Corp. v. Thermo-Rite Co.*, J.E. 97-2221 (C.S.), and *Argos Films v. Ciné 360 inc.*, [1991] R.J.Q. 1602 (C.A.)) which refer to Article 3148 *C.C.Q.* in the context of homologation motions brought under Article 949 *C.C.P.* Neither offers any substantial views about the relationship between these two provisions.

(3) a fault was committed in Quebec, damage was suffered in Quebec, an injurious act occurred in Quebec or one of the obligations arising from a contract was to be performed in Quebec;

(4) the parties have by agreement submitted to it all existing or future disputes between themselves arising out of a specified legal relationship;

(5) the defendant submits to its jurisdiction.

However, a Quebec authority has no jurisdiction where the parties, by agreement, have chosen to submit all existing or future disputes between themselves relating to a specified legal relationship to a foreign authority or to an arbitrator, unless the defendant submits to the jurisdiction of the Quebec authority. [Emphasis added]

As for the balance of the provisions under Book VII, Title II, Article 950(6) *C.C.P.* states that one of the possible objections against the recognition and execution of a foreign arbitral award in Québec is its setting aside or suspension "by a competent authority of the place or pursuant to the laws of the place in which the arbitration award was made." Article 951 *C.C.P.* adds that the motion for homologation may be postponed if the competent authority referred to in Article 950(6) *C.C.P.* has made an application to have the award set aside. The content of both of these articles is in perfect harmony with the provisions of the New York Convention and the UNCITRAL Model Law.

XII. Confidentiality

A. CONFIDENTIALITY AND PRIVACY ISSUES

As noted above, a desire for confidentiality is a principal commercial reason driving many companies to use arbitrations to resolve disputes. Arbitrations are often considered private, in that non-parties may be excluded from the hearing and are not entitled to see documents produced in the course of the proceeding. However, under Canadian law, and indeed under many countries' laws and various rules of arbitration, arbitrations are not necessarily confidential.[303] Even where they are confidential, such confidentiality may be lost if, for instance, appeal proceedings take place in public courts.

While there is little Canadian case law on this point, decisions from other national courts suggest that confidentiality should not be assumed to apply to arbitration proceedings, particularly where there is a public interest in the

---

[303] The same is true of court-annexed mediation in Ontario. Such mediations are "without prejudice settlement discussions" but are not confidential without a specific agreement of the parties. See Ontario *Rules of Civil Procedure*, Rule 24.1.14; *Rogacki v. Belz* (2003), 67 O.R. (3d) 330 (C.A.), *per* Borins, J.A., at 339 and *per* Abella, J.A. (now of the Supreme Court), at 344-347; *Galileo Canada Distribution Systems Inc. v. Asian Travel Alliance Inc. et al.* (unreported, Ont. Sup. Ct., 26 May 2005, *per* Spies J.).

outcome of the dispute.[304] Appellate courts in the United States, Australia and Sweden have all concluded that arbitrations are not necessarily confidential.[305] Courts in England have recognized both the commercial attraction of private and confidential arbitration proceedings and the public interest for the courts to be open, even when arbitration matters arise.[306] Although the Court of Appeal for Ontario has understood the need for privacy in resolving disputes arising in a non-public business,[307] the Canadian case law does not provide significant comfort for those seeking strong confidentiality of arbitrations.

---

[304] See *Esso Australia Resources Ltd. v. Plowman* (1995), 128 A.L.R. 391 (H.C.), which involved a public body seeking a declaration that it could release information from an arbitration relating to potential energy prices, in the public interest. The High Court found no implied term of confidentiality in an arbitration agreement and raised the prospect of a public interest exception to any confidentiality. At para. 35 *per* Mason C.J.: "... I do not consider that, in Australia, having regard to the various matters to which I have referred, we are justified in concluding that confidentiality is an essential attribute of a private arbitration imposing an obligation on each party not to disclose the proceedings or documents and information provided in and for the purposes of the arbitration." And *per* Brennan J. at para. 1: "[A] party who enters into an arbitration agreement is not taken merely on that account to have contracted to keep absolutely confidential all documents produced and information disclosed to that party by another party in the arbitration."

[305] *U.S. v. Panhandle Eastern Corp.*, 118 F.R.D. 346 (D. Del. 1988); *Esso Australia Resources Ltd. v. Plowman* (1995), 129 A.L.R. 391 (H.C.); *Bulgarian Foreign Trade Bank Ltd. v. A.I. Trade Finance Inc.*, Case T-6-111-98 (Supreme Court of Sweden).

[306] See *Dolling-Baker v. Merrett*, [1991] 2 All E.R. 890 (C.A.); *Ali Shipping Corporation v. Shipyard Trogir*, [1998] 2 All E.R. 136 (C.A.); *Associated Electric and Gas Insurance Services v. European Reinsurance Company of Zurich*, [2003] 1 All E.R. (Comm) 25 (J.C.P.C.); *City of Moscow et al. v. Bankers Trust Company et al.* [2004], All E.R. (Comm) 193 (C.A.). Following the principles of the *Arbitration Act*, 1996, the English civil procedure rules have since 2002 addressed confidentiality of arbitration proceedings before the English courts. See CPR Rules 62.2 to 62.10 (enacted by *The Civil Procedure (Amendment No. 5) Rules* (2001), S.I. No. 4015 (L32) (U.K.)).

[307] *Mantini v. Smith Lyons LLP*, *supra* note 115.

From a commercial party's perspective, the objective of protecting critical information from disclosure to non-parties (and indeed sometimes from disclosure to the opposite party) must also be balanced against a corporation's other legal obligations, particularly its obligation to comply with securities laws. Disclosure of the existence of a dispute and its potential financial impact on the corporation may be required. There are other examples of conflicting interests, such as the need to disclose potential liabilities where assets or a subsidiary that are subject to arbitration are being sold to a third party. Although confidentiality agreements may seek to protect the use of confidential information obtained by a purchaser in a due diligence process, if the purchaser is a competitor of either the claimant or the responding party to the arbitration, disclosure may well cause commercial concerns.[308]

B. GENERAL CONFIDENTIALITY PROTECTION

To assess the protection afforded to the corporation's confidential information, it is important to consider the impact of the laws and rules governing an arbitration. In practice, however, much of the confidentiality protection afforded to parties must be found either in the arbitration agreement or in the arbitration rules chosen by the parties to apply to the dispute.

Only two Canadian provinces' domestic arbitration legislation require that the arbitration, or aspects of it, be confidential. The *British Columbia Domestic Act* incorporates, by reference, the BCICAC Rules for Domestic Arbitrations; those rules contemplate that "all hearings, meetings and communications shall be private and confidential as between the parties, the arbitration tribunal and the Centre."[309] The *Nova Scotia Domestic Act* contemplates that the hearing

---

[308] See *PanCanadian Petroleum Ltd. v. Nova Scotia Resources (Ventures) Ltd.* (2000), 301 A.R. 287 (Q.B.).

[309] *British Columbia Domestic Act*, s. 22 and BCICAC Rules for Domestic Arbitrations, s. 25.

and meetings will be private and that "all written documentation" shall be kept confidential except on consent of all parties.[310] Both of these provisions are subject to an agreement of the parties to the contrary. The *Domestic Acts* in Alberta and Ontario do not even require that the arbitration hearing must be conducted in private. The same is true of Québec arbitration law and the UNCITRAL Model Law, applicable to arbitrations governed by provincial international arbitration statutes.

Certain international arbitration rules provide for a confidentiality protection. Two examples are the LCIA Rules of Arbitration and the BCICAC International Arbitration Rules. Both require that the parties agree to keep confidential all awards, all "materials in the proceedings created for the arbitration" and "all other documents produced by another party in the proceedings not otherwise in the public domain" with exceptions where disclosure is required by law or to enforce or challenge the award itself.[311] By contrast, the UNCITRAL Rules provide narrow protection simply requiring that the hearing be conducted in private.[312] Similarly, the ICC Rules of Arbitration exclude persons "not involved in the proceedings" from the hearing.[313]

Other arbitration rules provide no general confidentiality protection at all. The rules for arbitration under the North American Free Trade Agreement (NAFTA) provide expressly that nothing imposes a general duty of confidentiality and that (with one exception) nothing precludes the parties

---

[310] *Nova Scotia Domestic Act*, Schedule "A," s. 18.

[311] LCIA Rules of Arbitration, article 30.1; BCICAC International Arbitration Rules, Article 18(2) and Domestic Rules, Rule 25, both of which is subject to the parties written agreement to the contrary. The ADR Institute of Canada's National Arbitration Rules, Rule 33, also creates general confidentiality protection, subject to expectations for judicial challenge or enforcement of an award, disclosure to specified professional advisors and otherwise as required by law.

[312] UNCITRAL Rules, Article 25(4).

[313] ICC Rules of Arbitration, Article 21(3).

from providing public access to documents "submitted to, or issued by" a tribunal established under Chapter 11 of the NAFTA.

The decided Canadian court cases do not afford strong protection for commercial parties. There is an implied undertaking among the parties not to use any information obtained from another party for collateral purposes, a principle that may apply to arbitrations.[314] However, for commercial parties it is usually preferable not to rely upon judge-made principles where express contractual provisions may be negotiated.[315]

The importance of upholding and promoting arbitration in Canada as an inherently confidential process is significant, given that "[c]onfidentiality is often perceived as one of the great advantages of arbitration."[316] Confidentiality is of particular importance to the players in some of Canada's most active commercial sectors, including the oil and gas industry as well as the technology industry, particularly when it comes to outsourcing agreements.

---

[314] The deemed undertaking rule in Ontario (R.30.1.01(3)) does not apply to arbitration proceedings. The common law implied undertaking, however, likely does: *Tanner v. Clark* (2002), 60 O.R. (3d) 304 (Div. Ct.), aff'd (2003), 63 O.R. (3d) 508 (C.A.), leave to appeal to S.C.C. denied, [2003] S.C.C.A. No. 192.

[315] This is not to imply, however, that confidentiality agreements will not be overridden by courts or arbitral tribunals. See *Adesa Corp. v. Bob Dickersen Auction Service Ltd.*, *infra* note 320; *Husky Oil Operations Ltd. v. Anadarko Canada Corp.* (2004), 354 A.R. 15 (C.A.); and *Aetna Insurance of Canada v. Mason and Co.* (1998), 236 A.R. 49 (Q.B.). A recent Alberta case held that an arbitral tribunal has jurisdiction to order an arbitrating party to produce information for review by the tribunal and possible production to the opposite party, despite written confidentiality obligations to a non-party: *Jardine Lloyd Thompson Canada Inc. v. Western Oil Sands Inc.*, *supra* note 43. The Court based its conclusion on Article 19 of the UNCITRAL Model Law, which grants the tribunal the power to determine its own procedure over the parties to the arbitration.

[316] Nigel Rawding & Karolos Seeger, "Aegis v. European Re and the Confidentiality of Arbitration Awards" (2003) 19 *Arb. Int'l* 483 at 483. Similarly, the UNCITRAL Notes on Organizing Arbitral Proceedings indicate that "confidentiality is one of the advantageous and helpful features of arbitration."

Often, disputes require the disclosure of confidential and proprietary as well as strategic information.[317]

Unfortunately, the law of arbitration in Canada does not offer such assurances, and will not do so until case law squarely addresses the issue of confidentiality. In the meantime, as one Canadian observer notes, we are all "well advised to explicitly opt for confidentiality, if this is in fact [what we] want – not doing so, may mean taking a leap of faith and hoping for the best."[318]

An example of a confidentiality provision may be found in Article 30.1 of the LCIA Rules of Arbitration, which provides:

Confidentiality

30.1

Unless the parties expressly agree in writing to the contrary, the parties undertake as a general principle to keep confidential all awards in their arbitration, together with all materials in the proceedings created for the purpose of the arbitration and all other documents produced by another party in the proceedings not otherwise in the public domain – save and to the extent that disclosure may be required of a party by legal duty, to protect or pursue a legal right or to enforce or challenge an award in bona fide legal proceedings before a state court or other judicial authority.

Alternatively, one could consider a provision akin to Article 13 of Schedule B (Expedited Arbitration Procedure) of the *Nova Scotia Domestic Act*. That provision reads:

---

[317] K. Nairn, "Confidentiality in Arbitration: An Overview" in *Confidentiality and Energy Disputes: Proceedings of a Conference Held May 29-31, 2003* (Canadian Bar Association, 2003).

[318] M. Lalonde, "Commercial Arbitration and Confidentiality in Canada" (2002) *Euromoney Publications*.

Confidentiality

13 All oral hearings and meetings shall be held in private and all written documents shall be kept confidential by the arbitrator and the parties and shall not be disclosed to any other person, except with the consent of all parties.

C. SPECIFIC CONFIDENTIALITY PROTECTION MAY BE AVAILABLE

Beyond the general protections of confidentiality, parties may seek specific protection for critical business information, such as trade secrets.

Consider a dispute over the wrongful appropriation of a chemical formula for a pharmaceutical or the use of a recipe for a food product contrary to a licence agreement. To protect further improper use, an arbitral tribunal may be asked at an early stage to limit disclosure of the confidential information only to those directly involved in the arbitration (recognizing the need to allow the opposite party to fully prosecute, or make full answer to, the claim). Or, a party may even seek to preclude disclosure to representatives of the opposite party and only disclose certain information to counsel and experts, on their undertaking not to use the information outside of the arbitration process.

While Canadian arbitration legislation does not expressly address this issue, some international rules do expressly permit a tribunal to take measures to protect trade secrets and confidential information.[319] Canadian arbitrators applying domestic legislation tend to consider such requests on strong evidence of a risk to business interests and may find the legal ability to make a confidentiality order in their statutory jurisdiction to control the process of the hearing, or in the specific arbitrations rules that apply.

---

[319] ICC Rules of Arbitration, Article 20.7.

D. LOSS OF CONFIDENTIALITY

Parties must be aware that even if confidentiality is agreed or imposed by the applicable arbitration rules, there are exceptions and there are ways that the confidentiality may be lost.

Public access to the courts, including all evidence filed, is fundamental to the Canadian judicial system. While there are exceptions mandated by statute in certain family and criminal law contexts, in commercial matters it is an unusual case that is not fully open to public scrutiny. Thus, where an arbitral award or documents produced in an arbitration are placed before a Canadian court, it is assumed that the award and the documents are public.

Accordingly, parties who decide to apply for formal enforcement of an award, to appeal or seek leave to appeal, or to otherwise challenge an aspect of an arbitration in open court run a clear risk of losing confidentiality. In some cases, it may be sufficient for the parties to agree that the material will be provided to the court and then returned to the parties following a decision (if the court is amenable). But if third parties are involved and protest, Canadian courts will not necessarily abide by the parties' agreement to maintain confidentiality.[320]

Finally, if a party commences court proceedings other than appeal or enforcement, confidentiality may be lost even where the arbitral tribunal has made an order or award with a confidentiality provision. And in one recent decision, an Ontario court ordered production of transcripts from a confidential arbitration. The court took into consideration the nature of the issues raised in the subsequent court action, which party put the confidential information into issue in the court action, the fairness to the responding party and to the witnesses in failing to override the confidentiality and the protection otherwise afforded by the implied undertaking rule. The court concluded that the

---

[320] *887574 Ontario Ltd. v. Pizza Pizza Ltd.* (1994), 23 B.L.R. (2d) 239 (Ont. Gen. Div.).

arbitrator's confidentiality order should be set aside to permit production of the arbitration transcripts, but only for the purposes of the court action.[321]

E. PRACTICAL SOLUTIONS

As is apparent, the protections afforded by the mere privacy of the arbitration hearing and judge-made rules are often insufficient to protect trade secrets, competitive information, intellectual property, and other types of closely-guarded business information. Accordingly, if the parties want to ensure confidentiality (in addition to privacy) of information in an arbitration, it is advisable to agree expressly on confidentiality as part of the original agreement. Such an agreement should specifically address key business issues such as trade secrets. Further, consideration should be given to granting the arbitrator the express right to impose restrictions on who can see information and to ensure that sufficient disclosure will be made in the arbitration (so that parties may advance their arguments fully), without compromising the confidentiality of the information to the outside world.

Public companies concerned about disclosure obligations should consider whether a confidentiality clause should be subject to any obligation at law to disclose or report the existence and nature of an arbitration proceeding. If the matter is not addressed in the original agreement, it may be sensible for the parties to attempt to agree on what will not be disclosed or to agree on how the dispute is to be described in any such disclosure (recognizing that an agreement may be hard to achieve in the context of a newly commenced arbitration).

Maintaining confidentiality may require the avoidance of open court proceedings. For that reason, parties may agree upon appeals to a private appeal

---

[321] *Adesa Corp. v. Bob Dickersen Auction Service Ltd.* (2004), 247 D.L.R. (4th) 730 (Ont. S.C.J. (Comm. List)).

panel, or may agree to arbitrate or litigate subsequent disputes under agreed confidentiality regimes, or may seek court- or arbitrator-ordered protection.

XIII. Selected Other Issues

A. LIMITATION PERIODS

1. Common Law Provinces

i. *Statutory Limitation Periods*

Limitation periods present problems for lawyers in general and in the arbitration context in particular. It is clear that limitations legislation expressly applies to arbitrations in most provinces.[322] Accordingly, it is critical to commence an arbitration within the time periods set out in the legislation and to do so in accordance with the terms of the arbitration agreement and the applicable arbitration rules.

Many of the *Domestic Acts*, including Alberta's and Ontario's, have a useful provision to save a claim in certain specified circumstances, namely

---

[322] *Alberta Domestic Act*, s. 51; *Saskatchewan Domestic Act*, s. 52; *Manitoba Domestic Act*, s. 51; *Ontario Domestic Act*, s.52; *New Brunswick Domestic Act*, s. 52; *Nova Scotia Domestic Act*, s. 54. See the decision of the Queen's Bench justice in *Babcock and Wilcock Canada Ltd. v. Agrium Inc.* (2003), 347 A.R. 107 at 114, rejecting the argument that the Alberta legislation applies only to courts: *Alberta Domestic Act*, s. 2(3). The Court of Appeal agreed (see *supra* note 1).

where a court sets aside an award, terminates an arbitration or declares that an arbitration is invalid. If the court does so, it may order that the period from the commencement of the arbitration to the date of the order is excluded from the computation of time for limitations purposes.[323] But this section does not assist in every case and there is no such provision in British Columbia.

One recent Alberta case that falls outside the scenario contemplated by the *Domestic Acts* demonstrates the importance of following the arbitration agreement and commencing the arbitration within the relevant statutory limitation period. The parties agreed to arbitrate "any dispute or difference" between them. A Statement of Claim was issued in the Alberta Court of Queen's Bench within the limitation period, but was not served (as is permitted by the Alberta *Rules of Court*). A notice of arbitration was delivered more than six months later, after the expiry of the limitation period. Shortly after, the court Statement of Claim was served. The defendant/respondent moved in court to strike out the Statement of Claim and for a declaration that the arbitration could not be commenced due to the expiry of the limitation period. At first instance, the Court of Queen's Bench held that the arbitration was commenced out of time and could not continue. This ruling was not appealed. The Court also concluded that the Statement of Claim should not be struck out, allowing the claimant/plaintiff to continue in court.[324]

The Alberta Court of Appeal, however, struck out the Statement of Claim.[325] The Court held that because the underlying arbitration was statute-barred and the parties had expressly chosen arbitration for the dispute, the court litigation must be dismissed.[326] The Court refused to save the court proceed-

---

[323] *Alberta Domestic Act*, s. 51(2); *Saskatchewan Domestic Act*, s. 52(2); *Manitoba Domestic Act*, s. 51(2); *Ontario Domestic Act*, s. 52(2); *New Brunswick Domestic Act*, s. 52(2); *Nova Scotia Domestic Act*, s. 54(2).

[324] *Babcock and Wilcock Canada Ltd. v. Agrium Inc.*, *supra* note 322.

[325] *Supra* note 1 at para 11. The Court noted that the right to arbitration was "extinguished through the expiration of the limitations period."

[326] *Ibid.* at para 12.

ings on the grounds of unfairness (arising from the failure of the arbitration claim), because the legislature specifically made arbitrations subject to the *Limitations Act.*

In short, the claimant/plaintiff commenced a court proceeding that was in time but contrary to the arbitration agreement, and later delivered a notice of arbitration that was out of time but complied with the arbitration agreement. The result was a claim that was barred both ways.

A party that commences a court proceeding and ignores an agreement to arbitrate may therefore run the risk not only of an application to obtain a (mandatory) stay of the court proceedings but also of the application of an expired statutory limitation period.

ii. Contractual Limitation Periods

In a given commercial agreement, a contractual limitation clause may extinguish a right to commence any claim at all after the expiry of a time period, or (less commonly) may have the effect of denying a right to arbitrate after a certain date.

Although Canadian courts will generally enforce contractual limitation or exclusion of liability clauses,[327] it may be worthwhile for a claimant to argue that the contractual time limits do not intend to bar a claim at all. In addition, some arbitration agreements require the arbitral tribunal to deliver an award within a specified time period. Under most domestic arbitration legislation,

---

[327] See generally, *Hunter Engineering Co. v. Syncrude Canada Ltd.*, [1989] 1 S.C.R. 426 and the cases interpreting it. Under Canadian law, an exclusion or limitation of liability clause will be construed strictly against the party relying on it and enforced according to its true meaning, subject to unconscionability: *Bow Valley Husky v. Saint John Shipbuilding Ltd.*, [1997] 3 S.C.R. 1210, at para 28; *Plas-Tex Canada Ltd. v. Dow Chemical of Canada Limited*, 2004 ABCA 309, at para 49-55. In the specific context of contractual agreements excluding liability after a specified time period, consider the meaning and scope of s. 22 of the *Ontario Limitations Act*, 2002, which provides that a limitation period under the Act "applies despite any agreement to vary or exclude it."

the time to render an award may be extended even if the time has already extinguished. But there is no general power to extend time limits in either the *Domestic Acts* (other than British Columbia's) or in the UNCITRAL Model Law.[328]

iii. Possible Impact of the Ontario Limitations Act, 2002 *on Arbitrations*

The *Ontario Limitations Act, 2002*, imposes a "basic limitation" period of two years, an "ultimate limitation" period of 15 years, and takes away the freedom of parties to "vary or exclude" the application of the Act with respect to *any claims* pursued in *court* proceedings. Many sections of the *Limitations Act, 2002*, however, do not appear to apply to mediations nor, arguably, to arbitrations governed by Ontario law.

Section 11 of the *Limitations Act, 2002*, entitled "Attempted Resolution," provides that if a person with a claim and a person against whom the claim is made have agreed to have an independent third party resolve the claim or assist them in resolving it, limitation periods do not run from the date the agreement is made until a) the date the claim is resolved; b) the date the attempted resolution process is terminated; or c) the date the party terminates or withdraws from the agreement.

It is not clear whether section 11 was designed to cover arbitration agreements. In order to rationalize the content of section 11, one could argue that the heading of this section makes it clear that it applies to mediations only. Yet surely an arbitrator constitutes an "independent third party" hired to "resolve the claim" and submitting disputes to arbitration is one form of "attempting to resolve" them.

---

[328] *Alberta Domestic Act*, s. 39; *Saskatchewan Domestic Act*, s. 40; *Manitoba Domestic Act*, s. 39; *Ontario Domestic Act*, s. 39; *New Brunswick Domestic Act*, s. 39; *Nova Scotia Domestic Act*, s. 43. The British Columbia legislation is broader, permitting time extensions in various circumstances: see *British Columbia Domestic Act*, s. 20. A claimant may argue relief from forfeiture, however, under applicable statutory and common law principles.

Given that the limitations law of Ontario applies to arbitrations under section 52 of the *Ontario Domestic Act*, perhaps the intention of section 11 of the *Limitations Act, 2002*, is to permit the parties to an arbitration or mediation agreement to suspend the application of the latter Act for a period of time, if they so choose. But this would only apply to arbitration agreements entered into after a dispute has arisen, and arguably section 11 goes further. If a commercial agreement contains an arbitration or mediation clause from the outset of the commercial relationship, then it might even be argued that section 11 means there is no limitation period in the *Limitations Act, 2002*, relating to actionable wrongs covered by that mediation or arbitration agreement. In that way, the parties would not have to be concerned about the application of section 22 which prevents them from varying or excluding its application by agreement. At a minimum, there is a point of clarification to the extent that section 52 of the *Ontario Domestic Act* may be inconsistent with the wording of section 11 of the *Limitations Act, 2002*.

2. Limitation Periods in Québec

The limitation period for contractual claims in Québec is three years, pursuant to Article 2925 *C.C.Q.* According to Article 2884 *C.C.Q.*, the parties may not agree on an alternative limitation period.

As previously noted, the limitation period for applying for the annulment of an arbitration award is three months after reception of the award or of a decision rendered under Article 945.6.[329] With respect to the homologation of an arbitral award, however, the *C.C.P.* does not specify a limitation period. The Québec Court of Appeal has held that, at least with respect to the decisions of certain administrative tribunals, the applicable limitation period for homologation is that provided under Article 2924 *C.C.Q.*, which states

---

[329] Article 947.4 *C.C.P.*

that a right resulting from a judgment is prescribed by ten years.[330] Since an arbitration award is in essence a judgment (save that it does not have the executory force of a judgment until homologated[331]) it would seem that this ten-year limitation period for the decisions of administrative tribunals should also apply to arbitration awards. One issue that remains unresolved is the exact consequence of the application of this ten-year limitation period for judgments, pursuant to Article 2924 *C.C.Q.*, to the homologation of arbitration awards. Clearly, when a judgment is rendered, the limitation period for execution is ten years from the date of judgment. However, in the context of the homologation of an arbitration award, it is unclear whether the ten-year period starts from the point of homologation or whether it starts retroactively from the time the award was granted.

3. Limitation Periods in Inter-provincial Arbitrations and International Arbitrations Seated in Canada

In the context of an international or inter-provincial arbitration there are numerous legal issues that arise when considering limitation periods. These issues will often need to be carefully analyzed. The first problem is, which limitations regime applies to the dispute? The question is important because Ontario and Alberta have recently reformed their limitations legislation to create a two-year general limitation period, while most other Canadian provinces remain at six years for most tort and breach of contract claims.

Common law conflict of laws principles require the characterization of limitations as either procedural or substantive in nature. If characterized as procedural, limitations laws would typically be governed by the law of the forum (here, the law of the seat of the arbitration); if characterized as

---

[330] *Barreau du Québec v. Greenbaum*, [2002] R.J.Q. 2327; in that case the court considered an application for homologation of a decision of the discipline committee of the Barreau du Québec pursuant to the *Code des professions*, L.R.Q. c.C-26.

[331] Article 946.6 *C.C.P.*

substantive, limitations would be governed by the substantive law chosen by the parties or determined in accordance with general choice of law principles under a province's conflict of laws rules. The Supreme Court of Canada held in 1994 that limitation periods are substantive in nature for conflict of laws purposes, in a tort case in an inter-provincial dispute.[332] Most Canadian lawyers appear to consider that the principle applies to contracts as well, although the Supreme Court has not determined the specific point.

While the Court's decision governs in some jurisdictions, some provincial legislatures have addressed the questions of characterization and applicable limitation periods. The *Ontario Limitations Act, 2002*, provides that for the purposes of applying the rules of conflict of laws, the "limitations law of Ontario or any other jurisdiction is substantive."[333] But in Alberta, the *Limitations Act*, provides that the limitations law of Alberta "shall be applied whenever a remedial order is sought in this Province, notwithstanding that, in accordance with conflict of laws rules, the claim will be adjudicated under the substantive law of another jurisdiction."[334] The British Columbia limitations legislation does not directly address the classification point but provides that if the law of another jurisdiction is applicable and the limitation law of the other jurisdiction is classified as procedural, a court may apply British Columbia limitation law or the other jurisdiction's law "if a more just result is produced."[335]

Scrutiny of provincial limitations and arbitration legislation is prudent, then, before deciding how (and in some cases, where) to proceed.[336]

---

[332] *Tolofson v. Jenson*, [1994] 3 S.C.R. 1022.

[333] *Limitations Act*, 2002, S.O. 2002, c. 24, s. 23.

[334] *Limitations Act*, R.S.A. 2000, c. L-12, s. 12.

[335] *Limitations Act*, R.S.B.C. c. 266, s. 13.

[336] There are other reasons to be careful: at least one provincial limitations statute (Alberta's) also permits a written extension of limitation periods, and at least one province's legislation (Ontario's) does not allow an agreement to vary or exclude the

B. COSTS AND INTEREST

Costs relating to arbitration proceedings can be broken down into two categories. The first includes the costs of the arbitral tribunal itself and usually entails fees paid directly to arbitrators as well as their travel and other expenses associated with presiding over the arbitration. Also included in this category are the administrative fees paid to the arbitration institution, should the parties employ one, and fees paid to interpreters, translators, stenographers, and clerks as well as facility costs. The second category involves the parties' legal fees as well as disbursements made by lawyers in the course of preparing for the arbitration. This second category also encompasses fees paid for expertise and expert testimony, witnesses' travel expenses and the cost of document reproduction and communication.[337]

1. Common Law Provinces

While it is common for an agreement to arbitrate to provide that the parties share the costs of an arbitration, the domestic legislation addresses both costs awards and interest. An arbitral tribunal under the provincial *Domestic Acts* has the statutory power to make an award of all or part of the costs of the arbitration.[338] It may also award interest, essentially in the same manner as though the arbitral tribunal were a provincial superior court.[339]

---

statutory period. See *Limitations Act*, R.S.A. 2000, c. L-12, s. 7; *Limitations Act*, 2002, S.O. 2002, c. 24, s. 22.

[337] Redfern & Hunter (4th edn), *supra* note 51, at 396-400.

[338] *British Columbia Domestic Act*, s. 11; *Alberta Domestic Act*, s. 53; *Saskatchewan Domestic Act*, s. 54; *Manitoba Domestic Act*, s. 53; *Ontario Domestic Act*, s. 54; *Nova Scotia Domestic Act*, s. 56.

[339] *British Columbia Domestic Act*, s. 28; *Alberta Domestic Act*, s. 54; *Saskatchewan Domestic Act*, s. 57; *Manitoba Domestic Act*, s. 56; *Ontario Domestic Act*, s. 57; *Nova Scotia Domestic Act*, s. 57.

Practically, costs may be awarded to one party or to the other, or may be shared. As is the case for most Canadian litigation, an arbitration award for costs typically requires the unsuccessful party to pay either a portion, or all, of a successful party's reasonable costs. Under the *Domestic Acts*, costs consist of the party's legal expenses, the fees and expenses of the arbitral tribunal and "any other expenses related to the arbitration."

If no provision is made for costs in an arbitrator's award, either party may apply for an award of costs within 30 days of receiving the award. In making an award for costs under the *Domestic Acts*, an arbitrator may consider settlement offers made by the parties. Absent an award for costs or an express contractual provision addressing how the costs and expenses of the arbitration will be borne, the parties are responsible for equal shares of the fees and expenses of the arbitral tribunal and for paying their own legal expenses. Costs, including an arbitrator's fees and expenses, may be assessed or taxed in the same way as a law firm's accounts.

Interest may be awarded on financial payments ordered in an award and, generally speaking, may be ordered for the time before the award (pre-award interest) and between the date of the award and the date of its satisfaction (post-award interest).

The provincial *International Acts* contain no express jurisdiction to award costs or interest, except in British Columbia. In British Columbia, the *International Act* provides for both interest and costs to be awarded. Subject to any agreement between the parties, costs may be granted in the "discretion of the arbitral tribunal" and similarly, interest "may" be awarded.[340] Costs may include fees and expenses of the arbitral tribunal, legal fees and expenses, administrative fees of the British Columbia Arbitration Centre and "any other expenses incurred in connection with the arbitral proceedings."

---

[340] Sections 31(7) and (8).

The arbitration rules of some institutions, such as the ICC, LCIA and BCICAC, have express rules governing the payment of costs and expenses, including both categories of costs described above.[341]

2. Québec

Book VII of the *C.C.P.* regarding arbitration does not explicitly address the issues of costs and interest. However, an arbitral tribunal nonetheless has jurisdiction to award costs on the basis of Articles 944.1 and 944.10 of the *C.C.P.* Article 944.1 grants an arbitrator all powers necessary to the exercise of its jurisdiction as follows:

> Subject to this Title, the arbitrators shall proceed to the arbitration according to the procedure they determine. They have all the necessary powers for the exercise of their jurisdiction, including the power to appoint an expert.

Article 944.10 outlines the scope and extent of the arbitrator's jurisdiction:

> The arbitrators shall settle the dispute according to the rules of law which they consider appropriate and, where applicable, determine the amount of damages.
>
> They cannot act as amiable compositeurs except with the prior concurrence of the parties.
>
> They shall in all cases decide according to the stipulations of the contract and take account of applicable usage.

The parties are free to include a clause in their arbitration agreement that affirms, limits, or withdraws the arbitrator's discretion to award costs and such a clause will prevail. Parties are also free to specify precisely how costs

---

[341] LCIA Rules of Arbitration, Article 28; ICC Rules of Arbitration, Article 31; BCICAC Domestic Rules, Rule 38 and International Rules, Rules 37-38.

should be shared between them, or can subject themselves by agreement to Article 477 *C.C.P.*, which imposes costs on the losing party unless the court orders otherwise. Finally, it will often be the case that the institutional rules in question deal with the issue of costs.

Absent any of these circumstances, the arbitrator retains full discretion to decide on costs according to his or her assessment of the case, a discretion which is grounded in Articles 944.1 and 944.10 of the *C.C.P.* In particular, the Superior Court of Québec has indicated that the tribunal can award costs including extra-judicial fees as an award of damages under the first paragraph of Article 944.10.[342]

If there are no "stipulations of the contract" that deal with the apportionment of costs, Article 944.10 directs the arbitrator to take account of applicable usage. It is increasingly common in arbitral practice for tribunals to award costs against the party who loses on the merits,[343] as is the practice in litigation (a practice reflected by Article 477 of the *C.C.P.*). A tribunal could legitimately regard this practice as constituting "usage" and award costs against the losing party accordingly.

With respect to interest, courts in Québec have taken the view that interest constitutes a fruit deriving from the capital amount of damages and that the party awarded damages is therefore entitled, by right of accession, to an award of interest. Accordingly, arbitral tribunals implicitly have the power to award interest as part of their broad discretionary jurisdiction to determine damages under Article 944.10 of the *C.C.P.*[344] However, the scope of this reasoning has met with some controversy. In *Miller v. Comité d'arbitrage du barreau*

---

[342] *Société de construction des musées du Canada Inc. v. Acoustique Piché Inc.* (1994), 1994 CarswellQue 832 (C.S.).

[343] Emmanuel Gaillard & John Savage, *Fouchard, Gaillard, Goldman on International Commercial Arbitration* (The Hague: Kluwer Law International, 1999).

[344] *Renwick of Canada Inc. v. Investissement Admasa Inc.* (1990), 1990 CarswellQue 1473 (C.S.).

du Québec,[345] the court questioned its application to statutory arbitration such as that mandated for attorney-client cost disputes under the *Regulation Respecting the Conciliation and Arbitration Procedure for the Accounts of Advocates*,[346] pointing out that if a tribunal in this context indeed possessed such a power as part of its discretion, the legislature would not have expressly granted it in the Regulations as it had done. In that case, however, the court declined to resolve this uncertainty.

Arbitrators must apply the rate of interest specified by the parties; if no such rate is specified, an arbitrator can grant interest at the legal rate and the additional indemnity provided by law according to the scheme set forth in Articles 1618 and 1619 *C.C.Q.*

C. G.S.T. AND ARBITRATIONS

Seven per cent (7%) goods and services tax ("GST") is generally applicable on the provision of most services performed in Canada, including those in connection with arbitrations. However, in many instances, any adverse economic effect of the GST can be eliminated. For example, most participants in a commercial arbitration who are resident in Canada will be able to claim an input tax credit equal to the GST payable in respect of arbitration, tribunal or professional costs. In circumstances where arbitration or professional costs are incurred by a non-resident of Canada, such services should be qualified as "zero-rated" pursuant to relieving provisions in the GST legislation on behalf of non-residents.

In circumstances where costs are incurred by a resident of Canada who is not eligible to claim an input tax credit, GST costs will be in addition to any tribunal or professional fees.

---

[345]   (1993), 1993 CarswellQue 412 (C.S.).

[346]   R.R.Q., c.B-1, r.9.2.

Appendix

Canadian Legislation and Selected Arbitration Websites

Legislation	
Canada	http://laws.justice.gc.ca/en/index.html
British Columbia (subscription service)	http://www.qplegaleze.ca
Alberta (subscription service)	http://qpsource.gov.ab.ca
Saskatchewan	www.qp.gov.sk.ca
Manitoba	http://web2.gov.mb.ca/laws/statutes/index.php
Ontario	www.e-laws.gov.on.ca
Quebec	www.iijcan.org
New Brunswick	www.gnb.ca/0062/acts/index-e.asp
Nova Scotia	www.gov.ns.ca/legislature/legc/index.htm
Price Edward Island	www.gov.pe.ca/law/regulations/index.php3
Newfoundland and Labrador	www.hoa.gov.nl.ca/hoa/sr
Yukon	www.gov.yk.ca/legislation/pages/page_a.html
Northwest Territories	www.justice.gov.nt.ca/lcgislation/searchleg&reg.htm

Legislation	
Nunavut	www.nunavutcourtofjustice.ca/library/index.htm

ADR Organizations	
ADR Chambers, Inc.	www.adrchambers.com
ADR Institute of Canada (and regional offices in British Columbia, Alberta, Saskatchewan, Manitoba, Ontario and for the Atlantic provinces in Halifax, Nova Soctia)	www.amic.org/contactus.html
American Arbitration Association	www.adr.org
British Columbia International Commercial Arbitration Centre	www.bcicac.com
International Centre for Dispute Resolution	www.adr.org/International
International Centre for Settlement of Investment Disputes	www.worldbank.org/icsid/index.html
International Chamber of Commerce, International Court of Arbitration	http://www.iccwbo.org/index_court.asp
London Court of International Arbitration	www.lcia-arbitration.com
London Maritime Arbitrators Association	www.lmaa.org.uk
The Osler ADR Centre	www.osleradrcentre.com
United Nations Commission on International Trade Law	www.uncitral.org

About the Authors

Babak Barin is a partner at Woods & Partners in Montréal. He acts as counsel and arbitrator in domestic and international arbitrations. He has practised law in Toronto, London (England) and Zurich, Switzerland, and was Senior Legal Advisor and Team Leader at the Claims Resolution Tribunal for Dormant Accounts in Switzerland from 1999-2000. Babak is the Editor of *Carswell's Handbook of International Dispute Resolution Rules* (1999) and he has taught International Dispute Resolution at the University of Montreal. Babak is the Chair of ICCA Montreal 2006 Organizing Committee Inc.

Andrew D. Little is a partner in the Calgary office of Osler, Hoskin & Harcourt LLP. His litigation practice focuses on corporate and energy disputes, in arbitration and court proceedings. Andrew served as law clerk to Madam Justice Claire L'Heureux-Dubé of the Supreme Court of Canada in 1990-1991 and subsequently earned a B.C.L. at Balliol College, Oxford. Andrew has taught Corporate Litigation at the Faculty of Law, University of Calgary since 2000.

Randy A. Pepper is a partner in the Toronto office of Osler, Hoskin & Harcourt LLP. His practice is centred on corporate commercial litigation with an emphasis on arbitration and alternative dispute resolution. Randy has practised law in Canada and Hong Kong and heads Osler's International Commercial Arbitration/ADR group. He is on the Board of the ADR Institute of Ontario and the ADR Institute of Canada. Randy holds an L.L.M. specializing in arbitration and mediation from the London School of Economics.

Index